What
Car Dealers
Don't Want You to Know

Mark Eskeldson

Technews Publishing

Fair Oaks, CA

Library of Congress Catalog Card Number: 95-90352

ISBN: 0-9640560-1-1

Published by
Technews Publishing, a division of Technews Corp.,
7840 Madison Avenue, Suite 185, Fair Oaks, CA 95628

FIRST EDITION

1st Printing

Manufactured in the United States of America.

Cover Design by Paula Schlosser

DEDICATION

This book is dedicated to the honest car dealers and salespeople across the country who are tired of the greedy ones
giving their industry a bad name.

ACKNOWLEDGMENTS

This book would not have been possible without the co-operation of many people. My special thanks to the following: the current and former car salesmen who disclosed "the tricks of the trade," the victims of dishonest salesmen who called to tell their stories, and the investigators and attorneys working on consumer fraud cases involving dealers.

Thanks also to James Bragg of Fighting Chance® for providing information on dealer pricing/incentives, and to the dealers who provided cost information—and discounts—on extended warranties.

ABOUT THE AUTHOR

Mark Eskeldson is the author of the first hard-hitting exposé of the auto repair industry, *What Auto Mechanics Don't Want You to Know.* He has been involved in the auto industry for over 21 years, including jobs at several new-car dealerships, and is also the host of "Shop Talk: America's Radio Car Clinic."

Contents

Introduction

Are you one of those people who would rather have a root canal than negotiate with a car salesman? If so, you're not alone—most people rate that as the most unpleasant part of the whole car-buying experience. So, what's a person to do? Pay retail on the car you want—or buy a Saturn—just to avoid the hassle? Or is there a way for anyone, no matter how timid, to save a significant amount of money on the car of their choice?

The answers to those questions, and more, can be found in this book. And no, you're not going to learn how to go nine rounds in a knock-down, drag-out negotiating battle with a salesman. No one wants that (except the salesman). Fortunately, that's not necessary. The secrets of car dealers will be revealed so your next car-buying adventure will be not only profitable, but fun.

"Fun? You've got to be kidding!" No, I'm not. I put a few car-buying secrets in my last book, about ten percent of what's in this one, and a number of my radio listeners have used those successfully to get great deals on new cars. Here are some excerpts from a letter I received about a month ago: "...thank you for your book...A couple of weeks ago I went shopping for a new car...Using the information from your book I was able to purchase my new car at $450 below factory invoice (just over $2300 below sticker). I have never had so much fun shopping for a new vehicle as I did for this one. The information from your book was invaluable..." Signed, Edna from Citrus Heights, California.

In case you're wondering, Edna's new car was exactly what she wanted, including the color, and it wasn't last year's model from a clearance sale—it was a brand new, popular Japanese import. How did she do it? Simple: the right information and the right strategy, both contained in this book. (By the way, Edna's 49 years old and that was her fifth new car. And no, she's not a hostage negotiator or a martial arts expert.)

After hearing dozens of horror stories from callers who were ripped-off by unscrupulous salesmen, I decided to blow the whistle on extended warranty scams. No other car-buying book has done this before, and it's sure to make the dealers really mad: you're about to learn how much they cost—and where to buy them at a discount.

I also decided to expose the massive new-car scam of the 90's—leasing. Many dealers today are talking buyers into leasing because they aren't required to disclose all the details, allowing them to make huge profits at the expense of their customers. Don't enter a lease without learning the truth!

One last thing: you may encounter salesmen who will say that your information (on dealer cost) is wrong. If you have used the sources I've recommended, you can rest assured that they are accurate, so don't fall for that old line.

AUTHOR'S NOTE: The term "salesman" was used to improve readability and was not intended as a slight to the female salespeople of the auto industry. (Besides, I didn't feel comfortable throwing you in with all the "dishonest car salesmen.")

CHAPTER 1

Leasing:
The New Car Scam of the 90's

In February of 1995, ABC's *PrimeTime Live* did a show on auto leasing titled, "The Best Deal?" A female reporter went undercover, with a hidden camera, to see what would happen to several female "buyers" when they went shopping for new cars. Their stories, along with videotaped conversations with salesmen, revealed outrageous attempts to mislead and overcharge on new-car leases.

Out of ten dealers that were visited, five tried to talk the shopper into leasing instead of buying. In trying to convince her not to buy, one salesman said, "It's coming to the point where people are not even buying cars anymore." Another salesman said, "See, we learned a long time ago you don't buy things that depreciate, you lease them." And a third salesman said (convincingly), "It's the cheapest way ever to drive an automobile, period."

So, what kind of leasing deals were the undercover shoppers offered? Ones that *sounded* great—lower interest rates, lower monthly payments, and less money down. However, when the leasing deals were analyzed by several experts, a number of overcharges were discovered: $2,100 on one lease, then $2,600 on another one, $3,000 on a third, and a whopping $7,500 on a fourth. Out of five lease deals offered to the shoppers, all five contained attempted overcharges.

At one dealer, the shopper was told that the interest rate on a loan would be 10.5%, but the salesman said he could get her a 3% rate on a lease. However, when the lease numbers were analyzed, the actual rate was 8.4%—which wasn't disclosed verbally or in the contract. The attempted overcharge: $2,100. A second dealer pulled the same stunt: told her the rate on a loan was 7.75% compared to 3% on a lease, then wrote up her lease based on 7.4% (which wasn't disclosed in the contract). The attempted overcharge: $2,600.

Two other tricks were attempted by salesmen to get more money out of the *PrimeTime* shoppers: the "secret price boost" and the "disappearing trade-in." When one of the shoppers asked about purchasing a car that was advertised for $23,999 the salesman tried to talk her into a lease, then wrote up the leasing contract based on a price that was about $3,000 higher. Of course, the higher price wasn't disclosed in the contract.

The "disappearing trade-in" was attempted by two of the salesmen visited by *PrimeTime* shoppers. At one dealer, the shopper was offered $6,000 for her trade-in, but the salesman told her that she would be better-off if the trade wasn't put in writing. (He said that would lower the sales tax she paid, but no state charges tax on a trade-in.) Then the shopper agreed to put an additional $1,000 (cash) down, and the attempted overcharge got worse. Her lease payment was quoted as $364 (for 3 years) when it should have been only $153. (The trade-in and cash were not properly applied to the lease.) Total attempted overcharge: $7,500.

A second salesman also tried the "disappearing trade-in" trick on a *PrimeTime* shopper. After negotiating a lower price on a new vehicle, the shopper was promised $10,000 for her trade-in. However, the lease payment quoted for that transaction was $389 (for 3 years) when it should have been only $193. (Only $5,800 had been credited for her trade-in, not the $10,000 that was promised.) Total attempted overcharge: $7,000.

The 10 visits to dealers by *PrimeTime* shoppers resulted in 5 attempts to put them in leases containing overcharges with a grand total of $26,400. Besides the undercover incidents, *PrimeTime* also included interviews with several people who had recently leased new cars and claimed that similar things had happened to them.

Were these just isolated cases, or part of a much bigger problem? According to Florida Attorney General Bob Butterworth, it's a national problem. His office conducted a 2-year investigation of 26,000 auto leases, finding flagrant examples of fraud in about 10%. A few of the offenses: inflating price stickers used to determine lease payments, manipulating customers into leasing instead of buying, pocketing trade-in money instead of applying it to the lease, and under-valued trade-ins. Some people who signed leases thought they were buying their cars.

As a result of an investigation by Butterworth's office into Toyota's leasing practices in Florida, a settlement was announced in May of 1995. Southeast Toyota Distributors Inc. and 55 Florida Toyota dealers agreed to set up a $4.5 million fund to settle complaints regarding past leasing practices. The attorney general had accused the dealers of overcharging customers by not properly crediting down payments, rebates, and trade-ins on leases.

Florida is not the only state with numerous consumer complaints about auto leasing. Attorneys general from 22 states have formed a task force to come up with solutions for the growing problem of overcharges—and outright fraud—in auto leasing.

Automakers and dealers may claim that leasing is "the cheapest way to drive a car," but it's beginning to look like nothing more than a new way to confuse buyers so they can be ripped-off for a lot more money.

Leasing: "The Promise" & The Reality

As new-car prices crept higher and higher, making them unaffordable for many people, new-car sales began to slip. The "good old days" of the auto industry saw buyers trading in their cars for new ones every 3 to 4 years, but car owners are now holding on to their cars for about 8 years. Worse yet, since many can't afford the payments on a new car, they're buying late-model used cars instead. The automakers had to come up with something (besides cutting prices) to get people to buy more new cars, more often. Their solution: the savior of the new car industry, "auto leasing for the common man."

Previously used only by the wealthy and people in business, auto leasing was picked up by the major automakers as a way to get around the affordability problem and get people into new cars. The automakers' plan was to get people into new-car leases that would expire in 3 to 5 years; after that, they would have to turn in their cars and start over—hopefully with more new car leases. Ads shouted, "No money down and low monthly payments," and consumers took the bait.

When people asked how it worked, they were told, "Leasing is simple—instead of paying for the whole car, you only pay for the part you use." Rather than building equity in a car, people were told that it was cheaper to just pay the depreciation for a few years, then turn the car in and repeat the process. [That's not true if the buyer had planned to keep the car longer than the term of the lease.]

In a nutshell, leasing is *not* another way of financing

the purchase of a car, because the lessee (the customer) does not own the car, the leasing company does. When the lease is up, the car still belongs to the leasing company, but the customer can't use it anymore because he has to give it back—and if it has too many miles or excess wear-and-tear, he has to give the leasing company more money. Should the (now car-less) customer wish to, he can purchase the car at the end of the lease—for a substantial amount of money, of course (usually 40-60% of the original total lease amount).

In theory, auto leasing shouldn't have been a bad deal for someone who planned on buying a new car every 3 years, but something went wrong. Outright fraud is estimated in about 10% of the leases written in the last 5 years, and a far higher percentage contain terms and costs that a smart buyer would never agree to *if* he knew what they were—and fully understood them. How did things end up that way? The answer: greed and dishonesty. Since dealers were not required to fully inform lease customers, dishonest salesmen have been taking advantage of that loophole to make huge profits.

Why Leasing Scams Work

Many people, who would normally be afraid to do anything as complicated and expensive as leasing without getting the advice of their accountant, take the advice of their neighbor (who's been overcharged on every new car he's bought) or a car salesman (who gets paid to tell buyers how wonderful leasing is).

Despite the fact that they don't understand the leasing process, many buyers fall for it because 1) even a bad leasing deal can be made to *sound* good, and 2) they're told that "everybody's doing it" [a slogan also heard around drug users and teenagers having sex]. Then they trust *a car salesman* to tell them the truth and give them a good deal.

The dishonest car salesman now has an ideal situation: a customer who's convinced that leasing is "the smart thing to do," but has absolutely no idea what he is doing. Making huge profits off these buyers is easier than taking candy from a baby! Juggle the numbers, tell a few lies, and before you know it, the salesman has hit the jackpot.

What makes it so easy to pull a leasing scam is that there are no laws requiring dealers to disclose the interest rate, trade-in, or sale price figures that are used to determine the lease. Salesmen are free to make up any numbers that sound good because they don't have to put them in writing. The law only requires dealers to disclose the monthly payment and the residual (and maybe the excess mileage charge), but without the other figures, buyers can't tell what kind of a deal they're getting.

Before we get into discussions concerning the technical aspects of leasing, and how unscrupulous salesmen twist words and figures to overcharge unsuspecting buyers, we need to go over the basics of leasing.

Leasing Terminology

Acquisition fee: Fee charged by leasing company to buy vehicle and set up lease. Also called "initiation fee." Sometimes negotiable. Typical charge: $450

Cap cost/capitalized cost: The price of the car—what the leasing company is paying the dealer. Should be negotiable. The lower this figure is, the lower your payments will be.

Cap reduction: Any down payment and/or trade-in that reduces the final cap cost (total amount leased). An increase in this figure should reduce your monthly payment and cut your financing costs.

Closed-end lease: Leasing company assumes all risk for drop in value due to excess depreciation. Customer can just walk away at end of lease. (Preferred)

Depreciation: Difference between cap cost and residual.

Disposition fee: Fee charged at end of lease for turning in the vehicle. Negotiate this *before* signing the lease— only agree to pay an acquisition fee *or* a disposition fee, not both. Typical charge: $200-400

Early termination penalty: The price you'll pay to end your lease early. Ask what this is in advance—it could be thousands of dollars.

Excess mileage charge: Additional charge at end of lease for exceeding the mileage limit. Usually 15 cents per mile. Watch out for low-mileage leases—this charge can end up costing thousands of dollars.

Gap insurance: Policy to cover difference between balance owed on lease and normal insurance coverage. Needed in case of theft or total loss due to accident. Should be included in lease—insist on it.

Initiation fee: See "acquisition fee."

Lease rate: Monthly rate charged by leasing company, similar to interest rate. Includes both interest and profit. Lease rate = [final cap cost + residual] x money factor

Money factor: Used to determine lease rate. (This is usually negotiable—it should not be greater than the rate on loans.) Money factor = [annual interest rate ÷ 24]

MSRP: Manufacturer's Suggested Retail Price. This is almost always negotiable (except on Saturn vehicles).

Open-end lease: Lessee (customer) assumes risk for excess depreciation, might have to buy vehicle for more than it's worth, or sell at a loss and pay the leasing company the difference. (Avoid this type)

Residual value: What the car is supposed to be worth at the end of the lease; what the leasing company wants you to pay at the end if you buy the car (this is also negotiable).

A higher residual should result in lower payments, but don't buy the car at that price—offer less or walk away.
Term: Length of lease. Don't lease longer than 3 years, or excess wear-and-tear charges could be expensive.

The Mechanics of a Lease:
How to Figure Lease Payments

To set up a lease, three basic figures are required: the final cap cost (after any cap reduction), the residual value, and the lease rate (or money factor). All three are usually negotiable, although residual values are roughly set by industry publications like the *Automotive Lease Guide* (see Chapter 10). We'll show how this works by structuring a 3-year lease for a "typical" $20,000 car, nothing down, 8% interest rate, and a residual value of $10,000.

The cap cost is easy—it's the total purchase price of the car as sold to the leasing company (minus any cap reduction), which is $20,000 in this example.

The residual value set by the leasing company in this example is $10,000 (because the car will lose 50% of its value in 3 years).

Figuring the lease rate is a little more work. If you only have the annual interest rate, divide that by 24 to get the money factor. (In our example, 8% divided by 24 equals .003333) Now add the final cap cost and the residual together ($20,000 + $10,000) and multiply that number ($30,000) by the money factor (.003333). The result ($99.99) is the monthly lease rate.

Now we need to figure out the monthly depreciation, which is simply [the difference between the final cap cost and the residual value] divided by the number of months in the lease. Since the lease in our example is based on depreciation of $10,000 over 36 months, we just divide $10,000 by 36 to get $277.78 for our monthly depreciation.

All we have to do now to figure out the total monthly lease payment is to add the lease rate ($99.99) to the monthly depreciation ($277.78) for a grand total of $377.78. (This figure does not include sales tax,which is based on—and added to—the monthly payment. A tax rate of 7% would increase the monthly payment by another $26.44)

Our example of a no-down, $20,000 cap cost, 8%, 36-month lease has a monthly payment of $378. That's a straight-forward, no factory-subsidy lease. To lower the monthly payments, the residual would have to be increased, creating potential charges for excess mileage or wear-and-tear, or the customer would have to make a down payment, defeating one of the purposes of leasing—that of little-or-no money down.

Example: Leasing vs. Buying

If we were to buy the same car, using the same interest rate and price, the monthly payment on a 48-month (100%) loan would only be $110 more than the lease. Plus, we could reduce the monthly loan payment $50 by having a trade-in and/or down payment of $2,000. At the end of the 48 months, we would own the car and have no more payments—until the car falls apart. Compare that with trying to come up with $10,000 to buy the car at the end of the lease (after you've only saved $3960 in payments), or getting another lease and making payments forever.

I know, some of you are thinking, "Hey—you just compared a 36-month lease with a 48-month loan, that's not fair!" Sure it is. The guy with the lease won't have a car at the end of 36 months, so unless he wants to walk everywhere, he's going to have to lease another car. His payments will not only continue, they'll probably be higher the second time around. I just chose a 48-month loan to make the payments more affordable. Besides, leasing a car with a term longer than 36 months is such a bad idea that it shouldn't even be considered, so why use that in a comparison?

On the other hand, if you're willing to live with perpetual payments just to have a new set of wheels in your driveway every 2 to 3 years, and you don't really care how much it costs, then maybe you should consider leasing.

Short-Term Leases

Over the last few years, personal leasing has increased about 50% every year, now representing about 25% of all new car transactions. As more and more consumers became comfortable with the idea of leasing (without really understanding it), the automakers came up with an even better idea to increase new car sales: the short-term lease.

For automakers, the obvious benefit of a shorter lease is that people will have to turn in their cars sooner, giving dealers more opportunities to sell (or lease) new cars. Ford Motor Co. was the first to really push short-term leasing with the introduction of its 2-year "Red Carpet" leases, and the company quickly became the industry's leader in short-term leases as a percentage of new car sales. After seeing Ford's sales increase with this strategy, other companies are now giving it a try.

The "brilliant marketing strategy" of Ford may not deserve all the credit for the company's dramatic increase in short-term leases (and total sales). I recently discovered that Ford had been offering cash bonuses to its salespeople for writing Red Carpet leases. Typical bonus amounts were $75 to $100 per lease, but the bonus was increased if the new lease was a renewal. Some bonuses were as high as $500 per vehicle (and this was in addition to their normal salary and/or commission). The bonus program was started in 1989 and discontinued in April of 1995. [With incentives like that, no wonder so many Ford customers were talked into leasing.]

For consumers, there shouldn't be any financial advantages to a shorter (unsubsidized) lease—other than not having to do any maintenance beyond oil changes. Since the biggest depreciation hit happens in the first two years, and a straight lease payment is based on depreciation (and a money factor), the shorter lease *should* cost more per month than a longer one.

If a shorter lease looks cheaper, it could be a "low-mileage" deal (12,000 per year) that will cost a lot more if you exceed the mileage limit. Also, the leasing company could be requiring a large down payment, or the factory could be subsidizing the lease by bumping the residual and/or lowering the money factor. Any (or all) of these tricks can be used to lower monthly payments on a lease.

The Future of Leasing

Some industry experts predict that leasing will not continue to grow at the same rapid pace it has for the last four years. (As a matter of fact, leasing is considered by some to be nothing more than a "temporary solution to the affordability crisis.") One of the reasons given is that more disclosure will be provided to leasing customers in the near future, either voluntary or mandated by law, and the result will be a drop-off in leasing when people find out what the details are.

Another reason given is the flood of off-lease used cars that will hit the market by 1997, which could depress used car prices and cause losses for automakers who've been betting on higher residual values. Used car prices have been going up about 8-9% per year recently, a trend that can't continue much longer or used cars would be more expensive than new ones. (New car prices have only been increasing about 2-3% per year.) If used car prices fall, lease payments will have to go up since they're based on the future value of the cars.

It appears that automakers have made a "house of cards" built around leasing, new car prices, and used car prices. Leasing is promoted because too many people can't afford to buy new cars, demand has caused used car prices to go up—which lowers lease payments, and automakers claim that prices can't be cut on new cars without destroying the used car market—which would wipe out the automakers' leasing companies. Is the house of cards in danger of collapsing?

Advantages of Leasing

Leasing is supposed to have the following advantages: less money tied up in a vehicle due to little-or-no down and lower monthly payments, no trade-in or selling inconveniences, and protection against big losses due to depreciation (or buying a lemon). It's also a way for automakers to unload a lot of new cars at big discounts—without actually cutting the "selling" prices. They just offer subsidized leases with lower payments and watch their sales go up.

Phony Lease vs. Buy Comparisons

One of the tricks that's used to make leasing look "better" than buying is the comparison of the low payments on a factory-subsidized lease with the higher loan payments on a regular purchase at the retail price. What's not mentioned is that the lease payments are low because of a large, hidden discount in the price of the car. On a 3-year, 8% loan, the monthly payment drops $31 for each $1,000 discount in price. Any smart buyer (like you, after reading this book) could also take that big discount in a purchase, if they knew about it. [See Chapter 10.] Smart buyers don't pay the sticker price when purchasing, so don't let a salesman compare a discount lease with a purchase based on MSRP.

Another trick that's used to make leases look better is comparing short-term lease payments with the payments on an equally short-term loan that few people would ever choose because the payments would be too high. For example, to make our 36-month lease (from a few pages back) look even better, we could compare its $378 payments to the $627 payments on a 36-month loan. A more realistic choice would be a 5-year loan with monthly payments of $406. Think about that—only $28 a month more than a lease and you own the car in five years. Add a little to your payment each month and it's paid off earlier.

The "interest loss on up-front costs" is my personal favorite among phony arguments used to show why leasing is "better" than buying. A chart (or computer program) is used to show the customer how additional interest earned on the initial cash savings from a lease will reduce the overall cost (often by $500-800 or more). This argument is only valid if someone can afford the higher payments on a loan, so they would actually have extra cash to invest if they chose to lease. Since most people who lease cars for $25,000 or less are leasing because they can't afford the payments on a loan, the "lost interest" argument is phony because they won't have anything "left over" to invest.

No matter what any salesman tells you, an honest comparison of leasing versus buying will show that leasing not only fails to produce savings in the long run, but it often costs $600 to $1,000 more than buying for every 3-year period.

Disadvantages of Leasing

Some of the disadvantages of leasing include: higher depreciation (and sales tax) costs if a new car is leased every 2-3 years; higher insurance costs due to increased liability requirements and always driving a newer vehicle; and potential for expensive charges due to early termination, excess mileage or wear-and-tear. On vehicles where the residual was increased to lower the monthly payment, the lessee may end up paying more than the vehicle is really worth if it's purchased at the end of the lease.

When Leasing Makes Sense—
The Best Candidates for a Lease

The perfect candidate for a lease is someone in business who needs to drive a late-model luxury car in order to project a successful image, but doesn't want to tie up lots of cash that could be put to better use. As long as the vehicle is used for business, lease payments are usually tax deductible, adding another advantage to the low payments.

A recent ad for a 24-month lease on a Jaguar is a good example of this. The Jaguar has an MSRP of $54,480 and would cost about $1086 per month (for 48 months) with an 8% loan and $10,000 down. Using the advertised lease, the cash due at signing is only $1,398 and the monthly payment is $699. (This lease has a price discount of over $5,000 which cuts $208 off the monthly payment.) The low down payment on the lease saves $8,602 and the monthly payment is $387 less, resulting in substantial out-of-pocket savings during the term of the lease.

Of course, this lease customer would have to get another new-car lease after two years, but since he needs to drive a new car anyway (so potential clients will think he's successful), this could be the best way to accomplish that.

In addition, a person with this much "money to burn" is far more likely to actually invest his monthly savings than someone who is leasing a $15,000 vehicle, making the "investment income" advantage a legitimate one.

Car salesmen may claim that buyers with tight budgets can also benefit from low lease payments, but those are the ones who get into financial trouble when they can't make the payments or they try to get out of the lease early. For buyers who can't afford the loan payments on a new car, the smart choice is probably a good, late-model, low-mileage used car with an extended warranty. A $10,000 loan for 48 months at 10% would only cost $254 per month—and the buyer would own the car after 4 years. This makes a lot more financial sense than making lease payments (with higher insurance and sales tax costs) forever.

The Cheapest Way to Drive a Car

Paying cash is (almost) always cheaper than financing, so the less you borrow—and the faster you pay it off—the less it will cost you long-term. The biggest expense on a new car is depreciation, and since new cars lose about 50% of their value every 3 years, the longer you keep your car, the less it will cost to drive. (That's why leasing costs more in the long run.) However, at some point your car will start generating more expensive repair bills that might justify replacing it with a new(er) one. For most cars, the first 6 to 7 years are usually free of major repairs, so that may be a reasonable time to keep a car before considering the purchase of a new one.

For even greater savings, buy a car that's already 1 or 2 years old and you'll avoid the biggest depreciation hit. Cars just coming off a lease are great candidates for this strategy. A 2-year old lease car should be in excellent condition with low mileage, but its market value will be about 35-50% below original retail. Buying one of these—and keeping it at least 4-5 years—will cost a lot less over time than buying brand new models.

How to Negotiate a "Good" Lease

Should you decide to lease a new car, make sure you don't fall victim to any of the tricks in this book. Do your homework first to find out all about dealer's cost and incentives, then negotiate the cap cost (price) just as you would if you were purchasing the car. (Try for invoice or lower, settle for 2% over if that's the best you can do.) Find out what the residual value is and negotiate it as high as possible, then negotiate the interest rate as low as possible. Be sure it's a "closed-end" lease—"open-end" leases are too risky.

Walk out if necessary to get the terms you want and be sure to shop around before agreeing to anything; make them compete for your business. If you wish to purchase the vehicle when the lease ends, find out what it's worth and don't be afraid to offer (much) less than the residual.

Warning on Sub-Leasing

Some leasing customers learned the hard way about the high costs of terminating a lease early. Finding themselves unable to continue their payments, they tried to get out of their leases, only to discover that they would have to pay as much as several thousand dollars in penalties for early termination. Desperate for a solution, they turned to "sub-leasing" companies for help in finding someone to take over their payments. In many cases, they lost even more money when the companies ripped them off by collecting money but failing to make payments on the leases. People victimized by this practice often had their cars repossessed and their credit ruined. Because of this, auto sub-leasing is illegal in many states. It almost always violates the terms of a lease, giving the company grounds for immediate lease termination and penalties. *Don't let anyone talk you into sub-leasing a vehicle.*

COMMON LEASING TRICKS

The following tricks—and outright lies—have been widely used by dishonest car salesmen to overcharge consumers on leases. If you experience any of these, assume you are dealing with an unethical salesman. Then find a more honest dealership (and file a complaint against the dealer if the practices were outrageous).

There is no "purchase price" on a lease. Dishonest reason given for not disclosing cap cost; used to hide price increase.

The cap cost number won't affect your payment. Dishonest statement used to explain higher price than one negotiated by buyer.

There is no "interest rate" on a lease. Dishonest statement used to hide interest rate increase.

The secret price boost. After buyer negotiates lower price on car, salesman switches customer to a lease with a higher cap cost than negotiated price.

The disappearing trade-in. After buyer negotiates price on trade-in, full amount is not credited to lease.

The disappearing (cash) cap reduction. Buyer is talked into putting additional cash down to reduce monthly payment, but full amount is not properly credited to lease.

The phony low rate. Salesman quotes low interest rate on lease, then switches to higher rate. No rate disclosure on contract.

The phony "borrowing is cheaper" program. All-cash buyer is talked into leasing after being shown dishonest computer program "proving" that borrowing is cheaper than paying cash. [It isn't.] About 5,000 dealers in the U.S. purchased this program.

Inadequate disclosure. Failing to disclose any of the following in writing: cap cost (purchase price), cap reduction, interest rate, trade-in, residual, monthly payment, excess mileage charge, termination penalty, acquisition and disposition fees (if any), total due at signing.

Deceptive advertising. Ads for low-priced cars that don't exist (or limited to one car).

****

If salesmen are offering such good deals on leasing,
why do they have to resort to so many tricks
to get people to go along?

****

For a consumer checklist on leasing,
send a self-addressed, stamped envelope to:

"REALITY CHECK"
P.O. Box 19405
Washington, DC 20036

CHAPTER 2

The Truth About "Dealer Cost"

Car dealers, like any other large business, have a number of legitimate expenses that have to be paid out of the total gross profit of the entire business. Their expenses include rent, utilities, payroll, taxes, employee benefits, advertising, insurance, interest, equipment, office supplies, furniture, etc. Plus, a typical dealership represents an investment of at least $1 million (or more), and anyone who has that much money tied up in one business would expect to receive a decent return on his investment (this is known as "net profit").

However, all of the revenue needed to cover those expenses does not come from car sales alone. All car dealers have service departments, body shops, and parts departments that generate substantial revenues for the dealership.

To give one example, a dealership service department with a shop labor rate of $50 per hour and eight technicians (working at only 90% productivity) can easily generate $80,000 per month in gross profit from parts and labor. This figure is based on a conservative estimate of $15 per hour gross profit on parts installed by technicians, so the monthly total could increase substantially if more technicians are employed or more parts are installed. Now add gross profits from the body shop and parts department to the $80,000 monthly gross profit from the service department, and without counting *any* profits from selling new and used cars, there seems to be considerable revenues there to help cover the expenses of the dealership.

The purpose of the preceding (rather lengthy) explanation was to shoot holes in a common excuse used by some dealers in trying to justify the huge gross profits they attempt to make on new and used cars. It should be obvious by now that they don't have to cover *all* their business expenses just by selling cars—and you certainly don't want to pay a large part of their overhead just because you bought *one* car from them.

(On the other hand, if you don't mind paying $2,000 more than someone else for an identical car, you might feel better knowing that—because of you—the owner was able to surprise his wife with a trip to the Bahamas.)

For the purposes of the following discussion, we are only going to use the actual dealer's cost for one vehicle: the one you want to buy. As mentioned earlier, the dealer is free to make additional profits from other services and sales. He's even free to take advantage of other uninformed car buyers and make huge profits from their purchases; that's *their* problem, not yours. You just want the best possible deal on a new car, and you won't be able to do that without knowing how low to bid.

Many new car buyers pay thousands of dollars more than they have to because they don't know how much profit there is in a sale at the sticker price (MSRP). If a buyer doesn't know, and he makes a low offer anyway, the salesman will say, "We couldn't possibly sell at that price—why, that's below our cost!" The buyer falls for it, increases his offer $1,000 or more, and the seller ends up making $2,000 to $3,000 profit on the car.

Dealer Cost--Percent Factor

Some car-buying books recommend using a "percent factor" in determining dealer cost. To arrive at the approximate dealer's cost for domestic vehicles using this method, subtract the following percentages from the list price (MSRP):

Mini-compact	6-9%
Subcompact	10%
Compact	12-13%
Mid-size	16-17%
Full-size	18-19%
Trucks, vans, Luxury models	20-21%

Using the percent factor to figure dealer cost is not as accurate as using specific information published in *Edmund's New Car Prices, Pace Buyer's Guides,* or provided by other companies. The percentages are only approximates, with 1-2% translating into hundreds of dollars, and special packages or other promotional discounts can throw the percentages off another 1-2% (or more).

To further complicate matters, suggested list prices on options usually have a 15% profit margin, even on smaller cars that may only have a 6-10% margin on the base vehicle, making this method even more unreliable. (An actual example of this is included in the following section.) For these reasons, *I do not recommend using percentages*; use the actual "dealer invoice" figures instead.

Dealer Invoice

The "dealer invoice" amount is the price the dealer actually pays to buy new cars from the manufacturer, but it is not always the true dealer's cost on a particular vehicle. His real cost may end up being lower than the invoice amount if he is eligible for dealer holdback or any of the factory-to-dealer incentives, which will be explained later.

As mentioned in the previous section, dealer invoice is far more accurate than the percentage method, so this figure should be used as the starting point for determining the dealer's true cost. The following examples show the real profit margins on two cars (one mid-size and one compact) if they were sold at the list price (MSRP), including one option package for air conditioning, AM/FM stereo cassette, rear window defroster, light group, floor mats, etc.

	MSRP	Invoice
1993 Ford Taurus 4 Dr GL Sedan		
base price	$15,623	$13,455
GL Package 204A	2,412	2,051
Total	$18,035	$15,506
1993 Dodge Shadow ES 2 Dr HB		
base price	$9,804	$9,124
ES Package H	973	827
Total	$10,777	$9,951

Based on sales at the sticker price (MSRP), the dealer's profit margins were $2,529 on the Taurus and $826 on the Shadow. Had we used the percent factors instead, we would have thought the dealer's profit margins would be $2,885-3,066 on the Taurus and $1,293-1,401 on the Shadow. Since the percentage figures were off by as much as $400 to $500 from the actual dealer's invoice, they're obviously not close enough to be of any use.

Always look up the dealer invoice figures yourself, using one of the buyer's guides or services listed in Chapter 10. (I know this is hard to believe, but some dealers have been known to make up phony invoices—with higher numbers—to show prospective buyers.)

Once you have the real invoice figure, the next step is to find out whether the dealer is eligible for any additional money from the manufacturer that will lower his cost on the car below the invoice amount. Two of these programs are "dealer holdback" and "factory-to-dealer cash incentives."

Dealer Holdback

Dealer holdback is a specific percentage or dollar amount that the manufacturer holds back from a dealer until a car is sold, then his account is credited for the amount withheld. It's basically a method that's used to artificially inflate the invoice price, then hold onto some of the dealer's money for a while (interest free, of course) before giving it back. The holdback allows a dealer to make an additional profit (typically $400 to $500 or more) that's not reflected in the difference between invoice and sales prices.

If you've ever wondered why some dealers would be willing to show buyers the invoice, or why they would advertise certain cars for $50 over—or even under—invoice, now you know. They're not giving cars away because they're just really nice people (or really dumb businessmen), they can actually make money on those cars if there's any kind of holdback or dealer incentive.

Since most people don't even know what a holdback is, or how it affects a new car transaction, it's pure profit for the dealer. He doesn't have to negotiate with buyers

39

over it, and he doesn't have to share it with the salesman who sold the car. (Dealers don't even want their salesmen to know about holdbacks, so many of them don't.)

All of the domestic manufacturers (General Motors, Ford, & Chrysler) have dealer holdbacks based on 3% of the suggested list price (MSRP). This gives a dealer an additional profit of $600 on a car with a suggested list price of $20,000. Another way to look at this: A dealer could still make a $600 profit on that car if he sold it at the invoice price.

Some of the import manufacturers have begun offering holdback money to their dealers to help them remain competitive and profitable. Because this is a fairly recent development, and something the car companies do not want to become public knowledge, there may be holdbacks that are unknown outside the company. When in doubt, assume that a holdback of at least 2% (of MSRP) exists on the car you want and offer to pay factory invoice (or $200 to $300 over). Offer less if the dealer is getting an additional factory incentive.

Acura, BMW, Honda, Infiniti, Jaguar, Lexus, Mazda, Mitsubishi, Nissan, and Volkswagen all have dealer holdbacks of 2% based on MSRP. Isuzu, Saab, and Subaru have holdbacks of 3% based on MSRP. For Hyundai, Mercedes, and Toyota the holdback is 2% of the dealer invoice amount. The holdback for Porsche is 3% of dealer invoice. Volvo holdbacks are fixed dollar amounts: $800 for both the 850 Series and the 900 Series.

A final note: Holdbacks are not based on volume; the amount is the same at all dealers selling the same model.

Factory-to-Dealer Cash Incentives

Factory-to-dealer cash incentives are another way for dealers to make additional profits that would not be reflected in the spread between the dealer invoice and the sales price. These incentives are always tied to specific models, to help increase sales of slow-moving cars that are causing inventories to rise. Like holdback money, the dealer's account is credited for the appropriate amount after the car is sold.

Factory-to-dealer incentives differ from holdbacks in two ways. They usually have an expiration date and their value may be tied to volume—the more a dealer sells of a particular model, the higher the incentive paid on all of those cars sold during the program. This is the ideal situation for a buyer; a dealer can actually make a lot more money on cars that have already been sold, just by selling one more—even if he has to sell it for a price that is far below dealer invoice.

Sometimes factory-to-dealer incentives are publicized in an effort to drive potential buyers into the showrooms, using ads proclaiming big savings—a "limited time offer," of course. When this is done, the customer actually gets part (or all) of the incentive.

However, the manufacturer may decide not to publicize an incentive, leaving it to the individual dealers to make their own decisions concerning publicizing or sharing the incentives with buyers. As you would expect, when given the choice, dealers often decide to keep most (or all) of the money for themselves.

When an incentive program is not made public, dealers are not required to share the money with buyers, so don't expect them to volunteer the information. They may not even tell their salesmen, because if they did, their salesmen might start accepting lower offers.

The dollar amounts of dealer incentives vary and are changed periodically, so consumers need to call a service that keeps track of current dealer invoices, rebates, and incentives (like Fighting Chance®—see Chapter 10). Typical incentives range from $300 to $2,000 (or more) per car, which is additional profit for the dealer, so this information is crucial if you want to get the best deal on a new car.

To give a few examples, the following factory-to-dealer incentives on 1995 models were in effect on 2/27/95:

Ford Windstar	0-$600*
Isuzu Pickup	$1,000
Isuzu Trooper	$750
Mitsubishi Diamante	
Wagon	$4,000
LS Sedan	$3,500
Oldsmobile Cutlass	
Supreme Conv.	$500
Subaru Impreza	$750-1,250
Subaru Legacy	$600-1,000
*based on number sold	

Carryover Allowances

Have you ever seen those "year-end clearance sales" put on by dealers and wondered how they can make such drastic price reductions on new cars? If you thought dealers were losing money by "slashing prices thousands of dollars" just to get rid of last year's models, don't worry—they're not. Those year-end sales are always accompanied by some type of factory-to-dealer incentive to help them clear their lots, making way for the new models.

General Motors and Ford both have a regular incentive program just for year-end sales, called a "carryover allowance." When the new models come out, dealers receive a credit for 5% of the suggested list price (MSRP) on every unsold new vehicle that just became "last year's model." The carryover allowance for GM and Ford applies to all of their models (with the possible exception of some best-sellers), resulting in a substantial drop in the dealer's cost on leftover cars.

Other manufacturers who may not have a regular carryover allowance program usually have some type of factory-to-dealer cash incentive to help get rid of unsold cars. If they failed to do this, orders for new models would be greatly reduced because dealers' lots would still have too many unsold cars.

End-of-the-year dealer incentives are usually publicized, but in some cases a manufacturer may let its dealers decide how much of the incentive to share with buyers and whether to publicize it at all. If the dealer wants to keep most (or all) of the money to himself, his salesmen may not know how much the incentive is worth. Because of this, buyers should use a service to find out what incentives are available (see Chapter 10) before they start negotiating.

To show how these can reduce a dealer's cost, the following factory-to-dealer incentives were still in effect as of 2/27/94 on unsold 1994 models (six months after the new models were introduced):

Cadillac DeVille, Seville, Eldorado	$1,500
Isuzu Trooper	$1,250
Pickup	$1,000
Rodeo 4wd	$1,000
Mitsubishi Galant	$1,250-1,500
Diamante Wgn	$4,000
3000GT	$2,500-4,000
Subaru Legacy	$750-1,500
Impreza	$700-1,500
Suzuki Sidekick 2 Dr	$500
Sidekick 4 Dr	$300-500

Dealer Incentives
vs. Customer Rebates

The factory-to-dealer incentives discussed in this chapter are separate from any customer incentives, commonly called "customer rebates." Customer rebates always belong to the buyer and are not negotiable. However, car buyers are sometimes offered a choice between the rebate or below-market factory financing (see Chapter 6).

Both types of incentives—dealer and customer—may not apply to cars that are special-ordered. Customer rebate programs usually require buyers to purchase cars from a dealer's stock, and dealer incentives may expire before the car can be delivered. In this case, the dealer's actual cost on a car may be higher if it's special-ordered, and if a substantial customer rebate no longer applies, that new car could cost thousands more than one that's in stock.

National Advertising Charges

One thing to watch out for is the addition of a "national advertising charge" to either the dealer invoice or the final sales contract. If a dealer can get away with it, he may try to charge you as much as 1-2% of the sales price for advertising. These charges do not belong on the dealer invoice, so don't pay them!

Advertising is a normal business expense, just like rent or employee benefits, but dealers wouldn't dare to add those expenses to the price of a new car. (WalMart doesn't tack on a charge for advertising when they sell a television set, and dealers shouldn't, either.) The only reason some dealers try this is that they usually get away with it, and when they do, it's pure profit.

In a number of states, it is illegal for automakers to force dealers to pay into a cooperative advertising fund.

There are now several lawsuits (filed by dealers) against General Motors over its advertising funds, so whether it's legal or not, some dealers disagree with it—and you should, too.

Some new car dealers have been the subjects of civil lawsuits for typing advertising charges on their factory (dealer) invoices and telling buyers that the charges were part of their invoice cost. Don't fall for this trick.

Floor Plan Charges

Floor plan charges are the interest costs incurred by the dealer for financing the new cars on his lot, typically at a rate of 0.7-0.8% per month based on the dealer invoice price. Some dealers try to add this onto the sales contract (just like "national advertising charges"), using it as an excuse not to accept a low offer—"Mr. Smith, we couldn't possibly sell at that price. We've paid over $700 in interest on that car." Don't fall for this—tell them you're not going to pay it.

Interest on a business loan is just another normal business expense, one that shouldn't be added to a customer's final bill. Once again, WalMart doesn't add an interest (or "floor plan") charge to someone's bill when they buy a television set, so why should car dealers?

As for the phony excuse that interest charges on a particular car have cost a dealer hundreds of dollars, maybe if he had done a better job of marketing—including prices that are more competitive—his cars wouldn't sit on the lot so long before they're sold. Why should you have to pay for his poor business practices?

CHAPTER 3

"The System":
How Dealers Make Money

Since the objective of most (if not all) dealers is to make as much money as possible, they need to have a plan. It's not enough to just advertise and sell as many cars as they can (practically everyone tries to do that, anyway), because a dealer only gets so many new cars to sell each year. Plus, he's not going to have an unlimited supply of buyers, so he needs to get as much money as possible out of every car he sells. That's where "the system" comes in, and if you don't know how it works, you'll end up paying too much for your next car.

How Salesmen Are Paid

A key player in the dealer's "system" is, of course, the car salesman. But why would a salesman care whether the dealership makes $3,000 on a car instead of $1,000? Because in most cases the salesman is getting a percentage of the gross profit on every car he sells. (The exceptions are Saturn salespeople, who are paid a straight salary, and a small percentage of salespeople generally working in other "one-price/no-haggle" dealerships.)

Instead of a salary, most salesmen are paid a commission which is usually about 30% of the gross profit (based on dealer invoice, not incentives) on every car they sell. This puts the size of their paychecks in direct opposition to the best interests of their customers, which could explain why the president of Land Rover once said, "you couldn't have devised a better pay plan if your intent was to screw the customer." No wonder car salesmen have a bad reputation—they're rewarded for gouging their customers!

"System" Training

Extensive training programs are used on an on-going basis to make sure salesmen don't miss any opportunities to generate a profit for the dealership. Seminars, audio tapes, videos, classes, clinics, and on-the-job training are all used to teach salesmen how to turn shoppers into buyers, and how to get more money out of every sale.

Entire businesses have been built around the training of car salesmen. A number of ads for sales training run continuously in trade publications, a sure sign that those companies are getting results. One ad claims that their training will increase the gross profit on each unit by $150 to $300 through F&I ("back-end") sales, promising "no fee unless you see results." Another ad promises to "build gross profit and increase F&I income."

So, whenever you're dealing with a car salesman, assume that he's a well-trained professional, even if he doesn't act like one (that, in itself, could be an act). Let your guard down, and you'll regret it.

A New Strategy:
Salesmen as "Trusted Advisors"

A new game plan for dealers is sweeping the country—transforming the image of the salesman from that of a "showroom shark" [I got that from CBS-TV] to that of a "professional, trusted advisor" or consultant. One of the goals of this new plan is to "take the emphasis off price negotiations," focusing on "value" instead. [Translation: "We don't like competition—it forces us to lower our prices. We want everyone to pay retail."]

I have two questions regarding this new trend: 1) Are the salesmen still being paid a percentage of the profits? and 2) After everything that's happened, do you really expect people to suddenly start trusting car salesmen?

Advertising

Before a dealer can sell a car, he has to have a buyer, so a number of advertising strategies are used to "increase foot traffic" in a dealership. Red tag sales, Labor Day sales, Presidents' Day sales, you name it, they're all designed to bring in warm bodies so the salesmen will have potential buyers. People are led to believe that "special values are available" because there's a sale going on, but the truth of the matter is that most sales are just gimmicks. Those prices—or better—are available any day of the week to a shrewd buyer.

The only time a dealer's cost is reduced (so he can pass the savings on to you) is when the factory comes out with a special dealer incentive; other than that, his cost is always the same, so he can sell you a car on Tuesday for the same price he offered on Saturday. But he doesn't want you to know that—he wants you to think that Saturday is the last day to get that "low price," so you'll be afraid to leave without buying the car.

One old trick that must still work (or they wouldn't keep using it) is real large print advertising a particular car at a real low price, then explaining—at the bottom of the ad, in real small print—that only one vehicle is available at that price. [Sure, it's a sleazy trick, but anything goes when you're selling cars! Besides, the ad really works. And it's legal. Don't forget the new sales strategy— they're "trusted advisors" now.]

Where the Profits Are

New car dealers have a number of ways to make money on the sale of a new car: the "spread" between the factory in- voice and your purchase price, the dealer holdback, facto- ry-to-dealer cash incentives, "back-end sales," and your trade-in. To wring the maximum profit out of each trans- action, a dealer will try to make a little profit—or a lot— from each and every piece of the car-buying puzzle.

The attempt to make a large gross profit based on the selling price of a new (or used) car is obvious to most peo- ple, even though few consumers really know how much profit is involved. Less obvious to many people is the $1,000 to $2,000 in additional profit a dealer can make by telling a buyer that his trade-in is worth less than it really is. (If a dealer offers more for your trade-in than you know it's worth, watch out—that's a sure sign they're making a huge profit on your new car.) Then another $500 to $2,000 in additional profit may be picked up in the "F&I" office by talking a buyer into paying for a lot of worthless and/or overpriced services.

The F&I Office: Back-End Sales

A dealer can make a lot of profit on the "back end" of a car sale by talking a buyer into additional items or services *af- ter* they've agreed on the price of the car. These sales are made by the finance and insurance (F&I) man, who's of- ten one of the highest paid salesmen in a dealership. If you're not prepared for his sales pitch, he can quickly add several thousand dollars to the price of your new car.

Typical high-profit back-end items include: dealer financing, extended warranties, rustproofing/undercoating, paint sealer, fabric protection, pinstriping, credit-life or credit-disability insurance, and dealer prep charges.

Unless the factory is offering below-market financing (or your credit is so bad that you can't get a car loan anywhere else), you will end up paying a lot more if you use a dealer to finance your car. On a 48 month $12,000 loan, you'll pay $274 more in interest for each additional percentage point (and most dealers will usually try to charge you 2% over the going rate, which will cost you $548 more in interest over the life of the loan). Don't fall for that old line, "It will only cost a few more cents per month; is that worth all the time and effort to arrange your own financing?" *Yes, it is.*

Have your car loan pre-approved through your credit union or bank before you start negotiating, and you'll save yourself a lot of money. Credit unions usually offer the lowest rates, but shop around before you make a decision. If nothing else, at least you'll know whether the dealer's rate is a good deal or not.

Extended warranties provide an excellent way for dealers to pick up extra profits—tell a few horror stories about expensive repairs, then offer to include the warranty in the car loan ("easy monthly payments"). How much profit does a dealer make on a warranty? Usually $300 to $500, but sometimes as much as $900. [Ouch!]

Never buy credit-life or credit-disability insurance from a car dealer; they're both grossly overpriced. If you do want either of them (and you probably don't need them), you can definitely buy them from your insurance agent for a lot less. Don't be pressured into buying these—it's against the law for a lender to require you to buy them before making a loan.

"Dealer prep" charges are a common way for dealers to pick up any easy $150 to $200 (or more) in extra profit. The factory pays the dealer for this service, so if he can charge you for it anyway, it's pure profit. Don't fall for this.

Rustproofing/undercoating, paint sealer, fabric protection, and pinstriping are favorite high-profit back-end items for the F&I office. They cost the dealer very little (usually 10-20% of what they'll charge you for them), and in many cases, they're unnecessary and/or totally worthless. Don't be tricked into paying for any of these.

Why pay $200-400 to rustproof a car that has a 7 year/100,000 mile corrosion warranty, especially when studies have shown that newer cars are far less susceptible to rust than older ones? A 1985 study of 5- and 6-year-old cars in Michigan found 20% with rust perforation. By 1989, less than 3% were found with perforations, and few of the cars inspected ever had rustproofing/undercoating done.

A number of automakers have recently come out against aftermarket rustproofing: General Motors, Saturn, Toyota, Nissan, Volkswagen, Suzuki, and Subaru. Some of them warn that damage caused by aftermarket rustproofing will not be covered under warranty, and the treatment itself could void the corrosion warranty.

Regarding "fabric protection," most upholstery fabric is already treated before it's put in a car, but if you want this done anyway, just buy several cans of Scotchguard® at the store (for about $10) and do it yourself. Don't pay $100 or more for something that might not even be done. And the same goes for "paint sealer" charges—in most cases this is totally unnecessary and definitely overpriced. Most new cars today already have a factory clearcoat, so any paint sealer charge would be a complete ripoff. Be sure to call the factory's toll-free customer service number to find out if they think either of these services is necessary before you agree to pay for them.

Final Notes

As you can see, there are many pieces to the car-buying puzzle and all of them are designed to make money for the dealer. Learn them, and you won't become a victim. If you get confused, and the pieces get mixed up, it will be easier for an unscrupulous salesman to take advantage of you.

In dealing with car salesmen, never forget that they are the trained professionals, and you're not. They're taught how to keep you there until you buy, and if that fails, how to get you to come back. They're taught how to turn a "no" into a "yes" and how to get a commitment to purchase out of someone who's "just looking." They're also taught how to get the maximum profit out of every sale. If you try to play their game, chances are you'll lose.

So do your homework, make an offer, then leave—with a new car, on your terms, or to make the same offer at another dealer. Dealers don't like low-profit offers, but they take them all the time. *They just don't want anyone to know*.

What Car Dealers Don't Want You to Know

CHAPTER 4

Tricks Salesmen Use

If you follow the negotiating strategies outlined in Chapter 11, you should not have to deal with a salesman to buy a new car. Unfortunately, some dealers will not allow retail customers to deal directly with their fleet or sales managers, in which case you should try another dealer. Only as a last resort should an inexperienced buyer go one-on-one with a trained, professional salesman.

Remember that almost all car salesmen are paid a commission based on profit—the more the dealership makes on a car, the more the salesman gets paid. Since a "good" deal for a buyer is a "bad" deal for the salesman, a number of tricks are often used to help salesmen sell more cars for higher profits. The most common tricks used by salesmen (and their managers) are described in this chapter; make sure you understand how they work before you start negotiating.

The Question

"The question" is a tool used by car salesmen to manipulate and control buyers, for the express purpose of getting a commitment to purchase. Instead of giving answers to a buyer's questions, a salesman will often answer a question with another question that is designed to trick the buyer into promising to purchase a car that day.

Unlike the salesman, who may not feel any moral obligation to follow through on something unless it's in writing, buyers can often be trapped into buying just because they answer "yes" to a question that didn't sound like a legal commitment. Some common trick questions: "If I can get you $3,000 on your trade-in, will you buy today?" or "Will you buy today if we can get your monthly payment down to $250?" When the numbers quoted are better than a buyer expected, those trick questions become very effective. Don't forget—they're designed to get a commitment.

You can avoid this trap by answering trick questions with your own questions. Whatever you do, don't say "yes" to any trick questions until you're ready to buy. Instead, use answers such as, "I don't know," "I'll think it over," "I might consider it," or just change the subject.

(If you want to have fun with a salesman, try this: Instead of answering his trick questions, turn the tables on him by using your own trick questions in response to his. Don't let on that you're joking. Some crazy examples: "If I buy right now, will you sell me the car at $900 below invoice?" or "If I buy today, will you give me $4,000 for my Pinto [or other worthless trade-in]?" In the unlikely case that you get a definite "yes" in response to a ridiculous question, tell him you'll think it over after he gives you all of the financial details in writing, signed by the sales manager. Just remember—you're not obligated to buy a car until you've signed a contract!)

The Trade-in Buyer

If a car salesman identifies you as a "trade-in buyer," you are in big trouble. Once you say (or even hint) that you will buy a new car *if they offer you enough on your trade-*

in, you are marked as a sucker who can be taken advantage of in many parts of the transaction and not even notice as long as your trade-in price is acceptable.

How this scam works is fairly simple—John Smith knows his trade-in is only worth $800 (retail), but he tells the salesman that he will buy a new car today if they will give him $2,000 for his old car. The salesman will then figure out a way to make $3,000-4,000 profit from John's new car purchase even after "giving" him $2,000 for his trade-in.

John will end up paying the sticker price (MSRP) on the new car, his interest rate will be higher, there will be a number of overpriced or worthless ("back-end") options added to the car, he'll pay $180 for "processing," $400 for "dealer prep" and "transportation," $900 for an extended warranty (that's only worth $400), $350 for paint sealer and fabric protection, etc.

When it's all over, and John has been thoroughly fleeced, he will tell all of his friends what a shrewd negotiator he is because the dealer paid him $2,000 for his old clunker. (Before he left, the salesman probably said to John, "Mr. Smith, don't tell anyone how much we paid for your old car—we wouldn't want everyone in town to think we're pushovers." Yes, they would!)

The Payment Buyer

The "payment buyer" sets himself up for a rip-off similar to that of the "trade-in buyer." After learning that someone will buy a new car *as long as the monthly payment doesn't exceed a specific figure*, the salesman structures the deal to wring the maximum amount of profit out of the buyer—all around the specified monthly payment. A larger down payment is required, the length of the loan is extended to five or six years, the monthly payment is raised "just a little bit more," the purchase price of the car is as high as possible, numerous overpriced and/or worthless options are added, etc. The buyer doesn't even notice that he's been fleeced—he's just happy his payment is "affordable."

The Deposit

In "the deposit" scam, a buyer is told by the salesman that *he has to attach a deposit to his offer before the manager will take it seriously.* (That's not true.) The buyer's deposit check is then "lost" to prevent him from leaving after his offer is turned down, giving the salesman more time to wear down his victim. "I'm sorry Mr. Smith, but it looks like they've misplaced your check. I'm sure it will turn up, but while they're looking for it, why don't we try one more time to put something together."

If this happens to you, tell them to call you after the check shows up, then leave the dealership immediately. You can always stop payment on the check later if they don't give it back.

We Can't Find Your Keys

"We can't find your keys" is a scam that works just like "the deposit." The salesman asks for your car keys *to have your car appraised while you're talking.* The keys (and sometimes the car) are "temporarily misplaced" to prevent you from leaving while they continue to work you over.

To avoid getting caught in this scam, always bring an extra set of keys with you when you go shopping for a car. If someone tries to pull this trick on you, tell them to call you when the keys show up, then leave the dealership immediately. Better yet, don't give anyone your keys unless you go with them.

Bait and Switch

"Bait and switch" is a common trick in the auto sales industry. In this scam, the advertisement describes a great car at a real low price, but when people arrive at the dealer to see it, they're told, "We're sorry, that car was just sold. However, we do have another car just like it for only a few dollars more."

A dealer is not breaking the law if their ad mentioned (usually in microscopic print) that only one car was available at that price, but if the original car in the ad never existed, they're using an illegal business practice. If you encounter this, leave immediately and find another dealer.

The Raise (or Bump)

"The raise" or "bump" describes the sales practice of continually coming back to ask for more money after a buyer has made an offer. First it's $500 ("Mr. Smith, we're about $1,000 apart on this deal, but we're willing to split the difference with you, is that OK?"), then it's $200 ("Mr. Smith, I'm working real hard to try and get this deal through for you. I think I can talk my boss into it if you can just go up another $200.", then $100, then $50, etc. As you can see, Mr. Smith was just "bumped" $850 higher than his original offer.

What's particularly outrageous about this practice is that it's probably used the most on people who are already getting a bad deal, even though the salesman claims otherwise. "Gee, Mr. Smith, you're practically stealing this car from us. Please don't tell anyone about the deal you're getting—I wouldn't want word to get out that I'm a pushover." Of course, Mr. Smith is convinced that he is getting a great deal, so he'll tell everyone he knows, which is exactly what the salesman wants him to do.

Lowballing

"Lowballing" is basically an outright lie told to a customer to get him to come in (or come back) to a dealership. This can be done on the phone, quoting someone a low price to get them to come in, then making up an excuse as to why they can't buy a car at that price. "We only had one left at that price, and we just sold it. As long as you're here, let me show you a similar car that's only a few dollars more."

This scam is also used to get a buyer to come back after turning down all of his previous offers on a car. "I'm sorry we couldn't come down far enough to reach an agreement today, Mr. Smith. We'll be able to lower the price on that car if you come back tomorrow afternoon. I'm sure we'll be able to accept your original offer." The sole purpose of this lie is to keep Mr. Smith from buying a car somewhere else, and the lower the dishonest price, the better it works. When Mr. Smith goes back the next day, the salesman has another chance to wear him down and get more money out of him.

The Turnover & The Closer

"The turnover" (or "T.O.") is what happens when a salesman realizes he's going to lose a sale (on his terms), so he "turns over" the buyer to another salesman. However, the replacement isn't just another salesman, he's "the closer." The closer may be the sales manager, or he may just be the best salesman in the dealership.

Unlike the poor buyer, who is exhausted from hours of arguing with the salesman, the closer comes in rested and with a clear head, ready to start all over again. It's just a matter of time before he wears down the buyer's resistance, who then agrees to pay far more than he intended when he entered the sales office.

Salesmen will sometimes "turn over" a buyer to get additional money out of him even after he's agreed to a real bad deal on a car. Once a buyer is identified as a sucker, another salesman is sent in with a different approach to milk the buyer for even more money.

The Four Squares

"The four squares" is an old trick, but it works quite well if the victim hasn't seen it before. Taking a sheet of paper, the salesman draws two lines, dividing the page into four squares. The salesman then asks how much the buyer would like to pay for the new car and writes his answer in one of the squares. The amount the buyer would like to receive for his trade-in goes in another square, the monthly payment the buyer would like goes in the third square, and the down payment in the fourth square. (No matter how ridiculous the buyer's numbers are, they aren't challenged at all—yet.)

The buyer is then asked if he would buy the car right there, for the terms he specified. Of course, the buyer says he would, so the salesman has him sign the paper and put up a large deposit ("the deposit"—another scam).

The salesman then takes the buyer's offer to another room. After a while, he returns, telling the buyer that his numbers won't work. The salesman quickly goes to work on the "four-square paper," reducing the trade-in, then increasing the purchase price and the monthly payment while the buyer watches nervously. They negotiate back and forth, changing the numbers again and again.

After leaving periodically to "get the manager's approval" (which doesn't happen), the salesman returns to work on the numbers again. The sheet of paper turns into a jumbled mess and the buyer is thoroughly confused. (That's the plan—confuse the buyer, then take advantage of him.)

Assorted Lies

The following is a brief list of common lies used by dishonest car salesmen:

"That price is good for today only."
Not true—if they'll sell it today at that price, they'll sell it tomorrow at that price.

"There is no discount—our new models sell at full price."
This is only true on Saturn vehicles.

"A small discount is the best we can do."
Try another dealer—most will give substantial discounts to knowledgeable and determined car buyers.

"I'm new in this business."
If this was true, he wouldn't want you to know. It's just a trick so you will let your guard down, thinking he's too inexperienced to pull anything over on you.

"The deal you're offering is below our cost (or we're just breaking-even)—you have to pay a little more."
Assuming you're unaware of the dealer's cost, the salesman uses this trick to get more money out of you.

"Someone just called about that car you're interested in— they want to know if it's still for sale. What should I tell them?"
This is just a cheap trick to get a commitment. Sometimes it involves a phone call while you're sitting there negotiating, but the phone call is usually from another salesman or his boss, not from a legitimate customer.

CHAPTER 5

Extended Warranties:
Extra Protection or Extra Profits?

"Mr. Smith, you really should consider getting an extended warranty for your new car. Just one transmission repair bill could cost you $2,500 or more, but you can protect yourself against major repairs with an extended warranty that only costs $1,100. And we can add that into your car loan, so it will only cost you a few more dollars each month."

Sounds like a good idea, doesn't it? You can have "peace of mind" for only $1,100. But is it necessary? And is that a good price? What if the warranty costs you $1,500 to $2,000? Can you get a good warranty somewhere else for less money?

In the last three-and-a-half years of hosting "Shop Talk," I have received many calls from consumers who were sold overpriced—and often worthless—extended warranties. For example, some people paid $1,500 for a warranty, then were charged (multiple) deductibles that added up to $400 or $500 for one visit to the shop. Others paid as much as $1,800 to $2,000 for the same coverage that someone else got for less than $500. It's time to expose the "dirty little secret" of high-priced extended warranties—they are nothing but an attempt to make huge additional profits off of naive consumers.

Do You Really Need an Extended Warranty?

If you're buying a used car, it may be a good idea (if you can get a good warranty for $600 or less). On a new car, maybe not—especially if you've done your homework and picked a model that has a good track record for repairs. Many top-rated models receive those ratings because they usually go for at least six or seven years without any major repairs, only routine maintenance.

New cars today (with a few exceptions) are very reliable, and their original warranty coverage is much better than that offered in the past. Before 1992, the import manufacturers were the only ones offering widespread coverage for 3 years/36,000 miles. The Big Three domestics had only covered their cars for 1 year/12,000 miles before 1992, when they increased their warranties to 3 years/ 36,000 miles to be competitive. [Isn't competition great?]

With original factory warranties now covering vehicles for at least 3 years/36,000 miles—and in some cases, 4 years/50,000 or even 5 years/60,000—any extended warranty that is purchased will only cover the period after the original expires. For example, a "5/50" warranty that is purchased to cover a car with an original "3/36" is really only covering the car for 2 years/14,000 miles. To make matters worse, if you happen to put more miles on your car than the average driver, you could easily exceed the mileage limit long before the time limit runs out. If this happens, the extended warranty becomes totally worthless. (Incidently, the warranty companies are hoping this occurs.)

Should a late-model vehicle require any major repairs within one or two years of the original warranty's expiration, those repairs can often be done for free under a "secret warranty" or "goodwill adjustment." This is especially true when the problem is fairly common, or is caused by an obvious factory defect. (Car manufacturers are required by law to track vehicle defects and to offer free repairs—or reimbursement—for problems that are above average in frequency.)

Since new cars today are (generally) quite reliable, the issue of whether to buy an extended warranty or not boils down to a financial decision. Do you need to "insure against possible loss" because you lack the resources to cover any major repairs? Or do you think the car you are buying is going to stick you with huge repair bills? (If so, maybe you should find a better car.) How much would the "average" new car buyer spend on repairs if he didn't buy an extended warranty? Read on, and you'll find out.

The Odds of Incurring Repairs—
Who Usually Wins the Bet?

Less than 30% of all new car buyers purchase some type of extended warranty. Are the other 70% getting stuck with horrendous repair bills that would have been covered? Probably not. Based on several studies into these warranties—and actual claims vs. cost data—the ones *without* expensive extended warranties usually come out ahead financially.

According to the administrator for the mechanical breakdown insurance offered by credit unions, their average claims for all policies they offer (ranging from two to six years) are only about $400 per policy. These policies are regulated by law regarding price and risk, so it's probably safe to assume that there isn't a huge profit margin built into their selling prices.

For cars with average or better repair histories, credit unions sell "5/50" plans for $460 and 6 year/100,000 mile plans for $510 (with $25 deductibles). Both of those prices include a 20% sales commission, netting the insurance company $368 to $408 to cover all administrative costs, claims, and profits. The company's statement regarding average claims of $400—which could end up being higher than their net sales price—is possible because insurance companies invest the initial amounts, generating investment income that is used to keep costs (and premiums) down.

The insurance company knows from experience that it's only going to cost—on average—about $400 to cover claims (with a $25 deductible). On one type of service contract sold by dealers, the average payout on claims was about $260 (due to a higher deductible that resulted in fewer claims). Whether a warrranty company has average claims of $260 or $400 per policy, it's clear that buyers who pay a lot more than those amounts are betting against the warranty company that their repairs are going to cost more. If warranty companies were to consistently lose in their "bets" against policy buyers, the companies would go out of business, so who do you think is going to win? The warranty companies, of course.

The Latest Warranty Gimmick: "Money-Back If You Have No Claims"

Consumers who doubt that their new car will need enough repairs to justify the cost of an extended warranty have been a "tough sell" for dealers—especially when the warranty is $1,500 to $2,000. To counteract this problem, some dealers are now offering buyers what they claim is a great deal—the offer to return the full purchase price at the end of the warranty period if there are no claims.

While this might sound like a good deal, it's really just a marketing gimmick to increase sales. And it's brilliant! Think about it: you give them a large sum of money for five or six years, and if you do have any repair problems, you won't file a claim because you want your money back at the end of the warranty period. Even if you do make it to the end without a claim, and you get your money back, you've made the warranty company an interest-free loan for five or six years. [This plan may appeal to those who intentionally withhold too much income tax from their paychecks all year, then get excited because the IRS is "giving them" a large tax refund—without any interest.]

This clever scheme works even better if the warranty has a clause requiring claims to be made within a specified time after the repair (for example, 30 or 60 days). If a car has a 3 year/36,000 mile factory warranty, a 6 year extended warranty is only going to cover the car for 3 years or less. Let's say your car needs a $600 repair in the fourth year, but you don't file a claim because you want a full refund of the $1800 you paid for the warranty. In the fifth year, your car needs another $600 repair, but you don't file a claim (you're still hoping to get your money back). In year six—if your warranty hasn't expired due to mileage—another repair is needed, this time for $1,000.

What do you do now? If you file the claim, you'll only be covered for the latest repair, not the first two that cost you $1,200. You won't get your $1,800 back and your total repair costs will be $3,000 (including the warranty). If you don't file the claim, you will get the $1,800 back (without any interest), but only after you've spent $2,200 on repairs. Had you put the original $1,800 in an account paying only 5% interest, you would have had over $2,200 to pay the repair bills.

In case you're thinking that a net loss of $400 to $500 on a warranty that costs $1,800 doesn't sound that bad, let's compare it to the purchase of a 6 year credit union warranty for $500 with the remaining $1,300 put into an account earning 5% interest. At the end of the warranty period, you would have paid nothing for (covered) repairs—no matter how much they cost—and your $1,300 would have grown to over $1,740. The $440 in interest almost covers the $500 cost of the warranty. Your actual net cost for warranty coverage in this example is only $60.

Those "money-back" warranties look even worse if there is a high deductible involved or if the repairs are more expensive. Worse yet, if the company goes out of business before you get your money back (this has happened to a number of independent companies), you're out of luck. One final warning: should you sell your car or trade it in before the time is up, your warranty—and your chance of getting a refund—may be gone.

Why Dealers Push Extended Warranties

Extended warranties can add significant profits to any car sale—that's why dealers push them so hard. In 1990, the New York State Attorney General's office did a study of service contracts sold by dealers. The study found that on GM-sponsored contracts, 76% of the purchasers paid $200 (or more) over dealer cost, 16% paid $600 (or more) over cost, and 4% paid $900 (or more) over cost. The study also found that on Toyota-sponsored contracts, 92% of the purchasers paid $200 (or more) over dealer cost, 24% paid $600 (or more) over cost, and 3% paid $900 (or more) over cost. [I guess some dealers can't resist an opportunity to make a bundle off an unsuspecting customer.]

> One of my radio listeners called in with a perfect illustration of the attempts to sell high-profit, over-priced service contracts. "Jane" had gone to a local dealer to buy a new car. After getting them to take about $2,000 off the sticker price (she learned that from one of my earlier broadcasts), she ended up in the finance and insurance office. When the "F&I" man told Jane that she should consider getting an extended warranty for $900, she looked him in the eye and said, "That's too much; I'll give you $450." To her surprise, he agreed—without any argument. (Even at that price, they probably made a profit of $150 to $200.)

As if they didn't already have enough reasons to push service contracts, one company came up with a feature that dealers are sure to love. At the end of the warranty period, dealers can receive 100% of the (unused) reserves held by the insurance company and all of the investment income earned by their individual reserve accounts. (In a nutshell, if you don't use up your warranty money, the dealers get it.) Of course, it's up to each dealer to decide whether to share any of the money with the buyers of the contracts, so some people may not be told that their contract has this feature. Also, this type of policy could create a conflict of interest if the buyer is not told and the dealer tries to avoid performing repairs under warranty to keep more money in his reserve account. [I know—you're shocked that I would even suggest such a thing.]

With so much money to be made selling warranties, it's clear that buyers' best interests will often take a back seat to higher profits for dealers. Don't believe that a high-priced warranty is a good idea just because the salesman (or manager) says so.

If You Decide to Get an Extended Warranty

Should you decide to buy an extended warranty after reading about the pros and cons, be sure to do your homework first. Buy a car with a good repair history and you'll not only save money long-term, but the price of your warranty will be cheaper, too. Try not to pay more than $500 or $600 for an extra two or three years of coverage, and insist on a deductible of $25 to $50 per shop visit. Compare the coverage offered by competing plans. If you think your mileage will be above average, be sure to get a warranty with high mileage and time limits.

Thousands of people have given their hard-earned money to independent warranty companies that went out of business without paying their claims. To keep that from happening to you, only consider policies backed by factory-sponsored plans or large, top-rated insurance companies. (Some of these are listed at the end of this chapter, along with my recommendation.)

Watch out for contract language stating that deductibles must be paid "per item or repair," instead of "per visit" to the repair shop, especially if the deductible is more than $25. For example, one visit to the shop where it's determined that your car needs three different repairs can cost you $300 if your policy has a $100 deductible per item.

Another thing to watch out for is a warranty that requires you to go to a particular dealer (or shop) for any covered repairs. If you happen to be out of town, or you just don't like doing business with the shop they've chosen, the warranty may be worthless to you. Insist on a warranty that will cover repairs done by any licensed repair facility nationwide.

To convince you to pay more for a factory-sponsored warranty, some dealers may say that credit union plans (and other less-expensive insurance plans) will require you to pay the shop for any repairs, then file a claim for reimbursement. This is no longer true — most of the large companies use a corporate credit card for immediate payment of claims, so don't let someone use this scare tactic to sell you an overpriced warranty. (And don't buy a warranty without a direct-payment feature.)

Two more tips on extended warranties, then I'll explain how they work and where to buy them for less: 1) don't buy one without shopping around first, and 2) don't forget to negotiate the price if you're buying one from a dealer.

Service Contracts vs.
Mechanical Breakdown Insurance (MBI)

"Extended warranty" is a term used to describe the two types of coverage available to buyers — service contracts and mechanical breakdown insurance. Although they appear similar on the surface, there are significant differences between the two in how they are sold and how much they can cost.

Mechanical breakdown insurance (MBI) is an agreement between the customer and an insurance company to cover certain repairs during a fixed time/mileage period. As an insurance product, the sale of MBI's is regulated by the Department of Insurance — for coverage and price — and can only be sold through licensed fire and casualty agents.

By law, these policies must have a cancellation clause giving a buyer the right to cancel within 30 days of purchase (60 days in California) and receive a full refund. MBI's are typically sold by credit unions, and since their prices are regulated by the government, they are not negotiable.

A service contract is an agreement between the customer and a dealer/manufacturer to cover specified repairs; it is not insurance. Since it's not an insurance product, there is no regulatory oversight of prices (except in Florida), so service contracts are usually priced significantly higher than MBI's. When a service contract is offered by the manufacturer and it merely extends the warranty past the original factory warranty period, it becomes a true "extended warranty." Service contracts are (usually) sold only by car dealers, and since dealers are free to set their own prices, they are negotiable. Cancellation policies are usually the same as those found in MBI's.

WHERE TO GET EXTENDED WARRANTIES (FOR LESS)

My Favorite: Credit Union MBI Policies

My #1 recommendation for extended warranties is to purchase a mechanical breakdown insurance policy through a credit union. These policies are available nationwide, they're backed by a number of large insurance companies, and they offer direct payment to any licensed repair shop. Coverage is basically the same as a typical service contract: bumper-to-bumper, except for routine maintenance and normal wear items (tires, brakes, wiper blades, spark plugs, etc.). Besides having only a $25 deductible (per visit), their new car policies also cover the following: towing up to $35, rental car up to $25, travel interruption up to $50, and tire/road hazards.

Credit union policies are priced according to a vehicle's repair history—the more repairs needed, the higher the price. Ratings go from 1 to 7, with 1 being the best cars (because they need fewer repairs) and 7 the worst. Cars rated 5 to 7 should be avoided, 4's are marginal, and those rated 1 to 3 should be OK. For new cars rated 1 to 4, the prices for a 5 year/50,000 mile policy range from $360 to $490. For a 6 year/100,000 mile policy (the most common), prices range from $410 to $510 for cars rated 1 to 3, and $590 for cars rated 4.

Used car policies are also available through credit unions for cars that are not more than six years old. For lower mileage cars (35,000 miles or less), a 2 year/24,000 mile policy costs $420 to $520 for cars rated A, B, or C. For higher mileage used cars (35,001-70,000 miles), the same coverage costs $480 to $560 for the top three rate classes. These policies also have the same deductible, towing, and rental car features as the new car policies.

Credit unions also have other plans with different time/mileage combinations. The above plans were mentioned because they are the most common, and also to illustrate the drastic price differences between their plans and those sold by dealers.

Sales policies regarding MBI's will vary among credit unions. While virtually all will restrict sales to members only, the only requirement for membership is usually a savings account with a minimum balance of $100—a small price to pay for saving so much money on the warranty. (Actually, they'll pay you—interest on your savings.) Some may also restrict sales to those who use the credit union for a car loan, but since credit unions often have the lowest interest rates on loans, this would probably result in even greater savings on a new car.

Any credit union can access MBI carriers, so even if your credit union doesn't usually sell these policies, they can get one for you. If you don't have access to a credit union, call the major ones in your area. Many are now interested in gaining new "members" (i.e., depositors), even if they have no professional connections.

NOTE: Independent insurance agents can also access MBI carriers for the policies described above, so check your local listings for an agent near you.

Ryan Warranty Services

Ryan Warranty Services is one of the oldest and largest independent service contract administrators in the country. (Several car manufacturers' factory-sponsored warranties are actually handled by Ryan.) Their contracts have no suggested prices and are only sold through dealers, so it's probably safe to assume that they are marked up fairly high. Be sure to do some serious negotiating (and comparison shopping) before agreeing to buy one of these contracts.

An article on service contracts in *Consumers' CHECK-BOOK* listed a dealer who promised to sell Ryan contracts to *CHECKBOOK* readers for $49 over dealer cost. To take advantage of this discount offer, call Carroll Fisher at Martens Cars of Washington (DC), (202) 537-3000. (You can order by phone with a major credit card.) Tell her you want the *CHECKBOOK* price on Ryan service contracts, then ask her to give you prices and other information by phone or mail. Prices range from $400 to $1,800 (depending on vehicle ratings and coverage desired) and are supposed to be less than comparable factory-sponsored plans.

GEICO Multi-Risk Insurance

GEICO is a large insurance company that offers mechanical breakdown insurance in addition to regular auto policies. Several important features of the GEICO MBI policy may not be found in other warranties: 1) A buyer purchases coverage (and is billed) for only six months at a time, so

73

if the vehicle is sold or wrecked—or if the buyer just doesn't want the MBI coverage anymore—he can terminate the policy at any time and avoid paying for unwanted coverage. 2) Multi-Risk is "all-risk" coverage— that is, everything is covered *except* for a brief list of normal "wear and tear" and maintenance items (tires, brakes, spark plugs, filters, etc.). 3) The policy can be renewed continuously, up to 100,000 miles—that's the only limitation. 4) The policy has a $250 deductible and is only sold to GEICO auto insurance policyholders (in most states).

Since GEICO is known for its low rates on auto insurance, the above requirement may end up saving you even more money when you buy a new car. To apply (or get a free rate quote) for auto insurance and MBI coverage, just call their toll-free number, (800) 841-3000.

Multi-Risk prices vary from car to car, but coverage on one mid-size 1995 model was quoted at $44 per year for the first two years, then $82 per year starting in the third year. In this example, five years of coverage would only cost $334.

Another Service of CarBargains—
Factory-Backed Warranties for Less

Buyers who use the CarBargains service to get bids on a new car can also request information on dealers who have promised to sell factory-backed service contracts at substantial discounts, usually $25 to $50 over cost. When placing an order with CarBargains, ask for the free information on service contracts. (See Chapter 12 for a complete description of CarBargains' services.)

I talked to some of the dealers who offer this service and they promised to extend the same offer to my readers, as long as they ask for the "*CHECKBOOK* discounted price on service contracts" when they call. They also provided me with pricing information for some of the service contracts they sell, and I've included that in the book so you'll have an idea how much they're worth if you go to buy a car without calling for prices and information first. [I'm hoping everyone who reads this book will be too smart to make that mistake. Do yourself a favor and call them *before* you go to buy your car.]

IMPORTANT NOTE

Please do not call these dealers *after* you've already purchased a service contract to find out if you got a bad deal — by that time it will be too late. If too many people do that, some of these dealers may withdraw their offers and ask that their names be left out. (That already happened with one, so now we can't provide any information on discounted service contracts for that car line.)

I've included price ranges so you can compare these to the range of contract prices offered by your dealer. All plans are factory-backed service contracts with towing and rental car coverage. Unless otherwise noted, all plans have $50 deductibles per visit. Contracts must be ordered within 12 months of new car delivery. Call for prices and ordering information. (Prices subject to change.)

Billingsley Motors
5050 E. Winnemucca Blvd.
Winnemucca, NV 89445
(702) 623-5005
Contact: Frank Crnkovich (F&I mgr)

CHRYSLER/DODGE/PLYMOUTH/JEEP/EAGLE(All)
"Maximum Care" — all models — no deductible
6-yr/75,000 mi. $825-900
6-yr/100,000 mi. $1350-1425

GENERAL MOTORS (except Saturn)
Buick, Cadillac, Chevrolet, Oldsmobile, Pontiac, GMC
6-yr/75,000 mi. $600-1100
6-yr/100,000 mi. $1000-1950 ($650-1150 w/$200 ded.)

Academy Ford Sales
13401 Baltimore-Washington Blvd.
Laurel, MD 20707
(301) 419-2700
Contact: Jeff Popkin or Scott Dinsmore

FORD/MERCURY/LINCOLN (All)
"ESP"—Extended Service Plan:
6-yr/75,000 mi. "Premium Care" $820* / $970^
6-yr/75,000 mi. "Extra Care" $685* / $835^
6-yr/100,000 mi. "Premium Care" $1520* / $2020^
6-yr/100,000 mi. "Extra Care" $1180* / $1480^
 *Cars, minivans, light trucks, sport utility vehicles
 ^Bronco, F250, 4x4, medium duty trucks

Topping Volvo-Nissan
5111 20th Street, E.
Fife, WA 98424
(206) 922-5505
Contact: Debbie Williams (F&I mgr)

NISSAN (All)
"Nissan Security Plus"—3 levels
6-yr/75,000 mi. $325 (Sentra) - $775 (Maxima/300ZX)
6-yr/100,000 mi. $460 (Sentra) - $1178 (Maxima/300ZX)

Jordan Motors
609 E. Jefferson Blvd.
Mishawaka, IN 46545
(219) 259-1981
Contact: Rod Halberda (bus. mgr.)

TOYOTA (All) "Extra Care" Coverage
6-yr/75,000 mi. $370 (Corolla) - $885 (Supra)
6-yr/100,000 mi. (0 ded.) $525 (Corolla) - $935 (Supra)

CHAPTER 6

Financing:
Facts & Fallacies

Making the wrong decisions in financing a car can easily
end up costing a buyer an extra $500 to $1,000 (or more),
but most people don't even shop around for a loan before
they go to a dealer to buy a car. Instead, they trust a salesman to give them advice (and a good deal) on the financing
phase of their transaction. And that's exactly the way car
dealers want it, because a large part of their profit from car
sales is generated in the finance and insurance office.

A smart buyer does his homework first, making sure
that the interest rate he ends up with is the best that's available. He knows exactly what he wants and how much it's
worth, and when he leaves the "F & I" office, he hasn't
bought anything that he didn't want before he went in.

Finding the Best Deals

Interest rates on car loans can vary significantly from one
lender to another, so be sure to check the rates available at
a number of banks and credit unions. Banks usually have
reduced rates on loans for customers who set up an auto-
matic-payment plan, and credit unions often have rates that

are lower than many banks. Most credit unions also have mechanical breakdown insurance (extended warranties) at prices that are hard to beat, so if you don't belong to one, it might be worth joining. (See Chapter 5.) Have an outside loan pre-approved before you go to a dealer to negotiate on a car.

When 8% Financing Is Better Than 3%

Whenever you see low-interest factory financing, it's almost always offered instead of a customer rebate or dealer incentive that results in a price decrease. Rates as low as 5.9%—or even 2.9%—may sound like a bargain, but in some cases it might be smarter to take the rebate and go with a higher interest rate. As the following chart shows, a lower rate will be worth more on a longer-term loan, and also on a loan with a larger balance.

<u>each 1% reduction in interest rate saves:</u>
3-yr. loan:	$16.50 per $1,000 borrowed
4-yr. loan:	$22.50 per $1,000 borrowed
5-yr. loan:	$28.00 per $1,000 borrowed
6-yr. loan:	$34.00 per $1,000 borrowed

For example, let's say we're offered a $1,500 rebate or 5% financing on a 48-month loan, and we need to borrow $15,000. The going rate on loans right now is 8% and we need to figure out whether to take the low-rate loan or the rebate. Using the number from the chart, first multiply the 4-yr. savings ($22.50) times the number of thousands borrowed (15) = $337.50. That's the savings for a 1% reduction, but we're offered a 3% reduction, so multiply that final number ($337.50) by 3 to get $1012.50. The 3% rate reduction is worth $1012.50 on a $15,000 loan for 48 months. In this case, the rebate would be a better deal than the low-rate loan, so we would take the $1,500 and get an 8% loan, coming out ahead by $487.50.

"Upside-Down" Car Owners

"Upside-down" is insider language for owing more on a car than it's worth. The most common ways for this to happen are: 1) paying too high a price for a particular car, 2) not having a big enough down payment, 3) the term of the loan is too long, and 4) the interest rate is too high. Unfortunately, most people don't even know they have this problem until they try to sell their car early in the loan, then they have to come up with additional cash (over and above the purchase price) just to sell it.

Trading in an "upside-down" car on another one just makes the problem worse, because the salesman will have to make sure there's a huge profit margin on the new(er) car to cover the loss on the trade-in. Now the buyer has been victimized again by paying too much on another car.

The only solution to this problem—other than coming up with extra cash to sell the car—is to keep it until the loan has been paid down far enough to bail out.

No Pain, No Gain:
The Sober Way to Finance a Car

I'm not going to beat around the bush—the intelligent way to finance a car is to make a down payment that's as big as possible, and then make large monthly payments. The less you borrow, and the faster you pay it back, the less your overall finance costs will be. An added bonus to following this advice is that you probably won't find yourself in the "upside-down" condition mentioned above. *Just remember: no pain, no gain.* I know a lot of people won't like this advice, but I named this section "The Sober Way to

Finance a Car," not "The Painless Way..." By taking the "sober" route to financing, you avoid the "hangover" of watching thousands of your hard-earned dollars go down the drain. The following chart shows how much interest can add up in different term loans:

$20,000 loan @ 9% (numbers rounded off)

	3 yrs.	4 yrs.	5 yrs.	6 yrs.
mo. pay.	$636	$498	$415	$361
total cost	$22,896	$23,894	$24,912	$25,963
total interest		$2,896	$3,894	$4,912	$5,963

$16,000 loan @ 9% (numbers rounded off)

	3 yrs.	4 yrs.	5 yrs.	6 yrs.
mo. pay.	$509	$398	$332	$288
total cost	$18,317	$19,116	$19,930	$20,771
total interest		$2,317	$3,116	$3,930	$4,771

As you can see, a bigger down payment and/or shorter term can save thousands in interest over the life of the loan. For example, on a $20,000 loan, choosing a 5-year term instead of a 6-year one saves $1,051 in interest, but the monthly payment is only $54 more. *A little pain, big gain.* Pocket the savings and apply them to the down payment for your next new car—after you've kept the first one for at least 6 years to get the maximum benefit out of owning. With a bigger down payment on your next new car, you should be able to get a 4-year loan—with payments close to those of a bigger loan for 6 years. Now you'll save $1,655 in interest just from the difference between 4-year and 6-year loans with $4,000 down.

Compared to the 6-year $20,000 loan, switching to a 4-year loan with $4,000 down (on the next new car) will save $2,847 in interest. *A little pain, big gain.*

You've just learned a recipe for financial disaster: pay more than a car is worth, put nothing down, and finance the balance for at least 6 years. By the time your loan is paid off, you will have wasted at least $3,000 to $4,000 and you'll probably be unable to come up with any money for a down payment on another car, so a salesman will put you into another 6-year loan (or talk you into leasing). You will then make payments for the rest of your life.

How to Calculate Loan Payments

The following chart can be used to figure out loan payments for varying amounts and interest rates. For example, to figure out the payment on a $15,000 loan at 9% for 5 years, just multiply the number from the chart ($20.76) times the number of thousands borrowed (15) and you get a monthly payment of $311.40. *Remember: borrow as little as possible and pay it off as fast as possible.*

	Monthly Payment per $1,000 Loan			
Rate	3 yrs.	4 yrs.	5 yrs.	6 yrs.
8%	$31.34	$24.41	$20.28	$17.53
9%	$31.80	$24.89	$20.76	$18.03
10%	$32.27	$25.36	$21.25	$18.53
11%	$32.74	$25.85	$21.74	$19.04
12%	$33.22	$26.34	$22.25	$19.55
13%	$33.70	$26.83	$22.75	$20.07

Financing Your Extended Warranty

A common mistake buyers make is deciding to get an over-priced extended warranty (or service contract) from a dealer because they can include it in the car loan, allowing it to be paid off with "easy monthly payments." For example, a $1,200 service contract in a 5-year loan at 10% will cost $25.50 per month, with a total cost of $1,530. If we bought the same factory-sponsored service contract somewhere else at a discount (see Chapter 5), we would only have to pay $700, and even if we had to put that on a credit card at 18% for three years, it would only cost $25.31 per month for 36 months—not 5 years. Total cost: $911 if we take 3 years to pay it off. By paying an extra $10 every month, we could pay it off in two years. Total cost that way: $839—a savings of $691 over the service contract in the car loan.

As you can see, a different approach to the service contract game can result in dramatic savings. One more example, the best one yet: If we were to pay cash for a warranty through a credit union, we would only pay about $500 or less. Our savings: over $1,000 compared to the service contract in the car loan.

Other "F&I" Deals to Avoid

Be prepared for a number of sales pitches from the finance and insurance salesman, because a dealer might make more money putting additional "stuff" on your contract than they make on the car itself. Rustproofing/undercoating, paint sealer, fabric protection, credit life/disability insurance, car alarms, and extended warranties are all big money-makers for dealers.

A car alarm that costs $500 at a dealer can often be put in somewhere else for $100 to $150, and extended warranties can be purchased elsewhere (or negotiated) for a reasonable price. The rest of the items mentioned above are simply overpriced and/or worthless, so refuse to buy any of them.

The "Financing Is Cheaper Than Cash" Trick

Beware of phony charts or computer programs that are used by dishonest salesmen to convince buyers that financing is cheaper than paying cash. It isn't. They just want to convince you to finance so they'll have another opportunity to make money.

For most people, paying cash will always end up costing less than financing, even when below-market factory financing is offered at rates that look too good to be true. That's because buyers who use the special financing are usually giving up a rebate or discount in the price, so after you factor in the higher price with the total interest paid over the life of the loan, it adds up to a lot more than someone would have earned from investing the total amount.

In addition, any investment earnings will be reduced by income taxes—at least 28% for most people—making the cash deal look even better. Since the "real" (unsubsidized) cost of financing is usually around 8-11%, you would have to make 12-16% on your investment to come out ahead of the cash deal (after taxes). Unless you're a loan shark, you're probably not going to make anywhere near that much, so the "financing is better" argument is a phony one.

Comparing Leasing With Buying

When comparing leasing with buying, be sure to include all leasing fees paid up front, any down payment, the total of all monthly payments (including tax), the residual, and any disposition fee. That's the total cost of a lease. The cost of buying is the total of all monthly payments, plus any down payment, fees, or taxes paid up front.

Beware of any comparison showing a big advantage to leasing over buying—there shouldn't be any.

Using Home Equity Loans for Cars

Ever since Congress ended the interest deduction for all installment loans except mortgages, some "financial experts" have been recommending that people use home equity loans to buy cars—just for the tax deduction. While the deduction would lower the cost of a car loan, I'm not very comfortable with the thought of mortgaging the house to buy a car. Should something happen, instead of just having the car repossessed, a person could lose their house in a foreclosure.

Besides the little foreclosure issue, there may not be much of an advantage to using a home equity loan to buy a car. Since equity loans are real estate loans, they often involve set-up costs that can total several hundred dollars (or more), wiping out any possible savings from the interest deduction. And the interest rate on equity loans is usually a little higher than car loans, making them even harder to justify.

My biggest objection to using home equity loans for buying cars is the strong possibility that many people would just get into trouble using them. After all, most people leasing cars today are only doing that because they can't afford the down payment and monthly payments on a loan. Without the shorter term of a car loan, many people would take a lot longer to pay off their car, driving up the total interest cost on the loan and possibly taking ten years or more to pay it off. Their loan could last longer than the car!

CHAPTER 7

Your Old Car:
Trade-in Tips

The best advice anyone can give on how to get the most money for your trade-in is: *Don't do it!* Car dealers "buy low and sell high"—that's how they make money—so don't be fooled into thinking that a dealer is going to pay you "fair market value" for your old car.

Any offer from a dealer that is significantly higher than the wholesale value of your old car is a good indication that you are paying too much for the new one. In this case, the dealer will just use part of the huge profit he's making on your new car to knowingly "pay" more than the trade-in is really worth. Never forget that you are dealing with a professional and if anyone is going to be taken advantage of, it will be you, not the dealer.

The following dealer ad is a classic example of how buyers are fooled into thinking they are getting a great deal: "We'll give you one thousand dollars, or more, for your trade-in when you buy a new car or truck. That's right, guaranteed! One thousand dollars, or more, for any trade-in, running or not. So drive it, push it, or tow it here today, and take advantage of this special offer!" This dealer is just going to make sure his profit on the new car is high enough to cover a worthless trade-in.

To get the best possible price for your old car, you must sell it yourself. I know this is an inconvenient and sometimes unpleasant experience, but the more your car is worth, the more money is at stake. A typical five-year old mid-size domestic car has a $1,200 difference (or more) between low and high retail values, and dealers are only going to pay wholesale (which is usually *at least* $900 less than low retail) on trade-ins.

As you can see, this can quickly add up to thousands of your hard-earned dollars going into the dealer's pocket. With this much money at stake, isn't the inconvenience worth the $1-2,000 (or more) you'll save? Even if it takes ten hours to prepare, show, and sell your old car for $1,500 more than a dealer would give you on a trade-in, that works out to $150 per hour—tax free! Few people make anywhere near this kind of money at their job, but they "don't want to be bothered" doing this when buying a car. Amazing!

Since the best deal for you is to sell your old car yourself, the following sections are included to provide some tips that will help you get the highest price for your old car. For those who insist on trading in their old car, in spite of the fact that they will end up with less money, a section is included at the end on trade-ins.

Research

Whether you are selling your old car, or trading it in, you need to do some homework if you want to get top dollar.

First, do some research to determine the approximate fair market value of your car. Start with the information provided in several paperback guides for used car prices (for example, *Kelley Blue Book Consumer Edition* or *Edmund's Used Car Prices*). These can be purchased at most bookstores for $5-10, or if you're lucky, your local library may have them.

Be sure to check at least two different guide books, because the prices given are not usually the same. *Edmund's Used Car Prices* lists current wholesale (what a dealer would pay for a particular car) and average retail, but no price ranges. The *Kelley Blue Book Consumer Edition* provides figures for two categories: "retail/good condition" and "retail/excellent condition," but no wholesale price figures for trade-ins.

For the purposes of determining the market value of a car, "good condition" means that a vehicle has no major defects or mechanical problems. The interior, body, and paint have only minor blemishes, and the tires have substantial tread remaining. Some reconditioning and/or minor repairs are needed.

"Excellent condition" means that a vehicle is free of visual and mechanical defects—it looks and runs great. The interior, body, and paint have no visible defects, and the tires are new (or like new). No reconditioning or repairs are needed.

After you have determined the "book" price range for your car, consult your local newspaper classifieds to see if there are any similar cars for sale in your area. Compare their condition, mileage, and equipment with yours, then take into account their book value and how long they've been on the market (to determine whether they're overpriced).

Actual selling prices of similar cars in your area will determine the true market value of your car, to a greater extent than the price guides, but it's still a good idea to look up the numbers, anyway. Knowing the approximate value of your car could save you from "giving it away" by pricing it too low. Don't try to compete with other cars that are advertised at "distress sale" prices, or are priced low because they're "lemons."

Preparing Your Car

Once you have figured out the price range for your car, have it inspected for safety and mechanical defects, then get estimates for any problems that were found. If your car received a clean bill of health, get it in writing to show prospective buyers. Written inspections from an impartial source can help you get top dollar for your car, especially if done by AAA. Inspections done by repair shops may or may not be taken at face value, depending on the buyer.

If a number of items need repair, determine which ones can be fixed without spending a lot of money. Expensive repairs done before selling a car rarely increase its value more than a nominal amount, because the "book value" assumes that a car is already in good condition. That's why it's a good idea to first determine your car's fair market value—so you don't spend $1,500 repairing a car that will still only be worth $1,800 when you're done.

Repairs that are safety-related or ones that will improve the driveability of your car are usually worth doing before putting it up for sale, especially if they can be done at a reasonable cost. After road-testing a car with bad steering or brakes, or one that runs poorly, a smart buyer will wonder why those problems weren't fixed and may assume the car needs expensive repairs. This will result in lower offers on your car, or worse yet, no offers at all.

Make sure all accessories, lights, and equipment are working properly. Check all of the tires, including the spare. If any of the tires need replacing, shop around for the lowest price on new radials, then replace them in pairs only (both fronts or both rears). A car with matching tires will look and drive better than one with three or four different brands.

Change the oil and filter, then check the coolant (antifreeze) in the radiator—if it doesn't look clean, flush the radiator and put in new coolant. Smart buyers will take a look at the oil and coolant to see if the car has been properly maintained, so make sure those fluids look like new. If the air filter is easy to remove, make sure it's clean, too.

In determining which items to fix before selling a car, keep this in mind: the most cost-effective repairs are the ones that make the most noticeable improvement for the least amount of money, so don't spend a fortune—you won't get it all back.

When you're ready to put the car up for sale, get a smog inspection and certificate so you can show potential buyers that your car is in good shape and it's smog-legal. As the seller, you are legally responsible for delivering a vehicle that (1) has all the required smog equipment, in working order, and (2) will pass inspection.

You can't avoid liability by selling the vehicle "as is" and telling the buyer that the smog equipment is his or her problem. I've seen vehicle sales unravel after-the-fact when the buyers took the sellers to court over expensive smog repairs. A seller could end up having to pay a buyer a large amount of money (as much as the sale price), or taking the car back (even if it's in worse condition), so make sure your car passes inspection *before* putting it up for sale.

Have the car detailed (or do it yourself) so the body and paint look as good as possible—make it shine! The interior should look and smell clean. Clean out the trunk. Don't forget: the fewer things a buyer finds wrong, the better your chances of selling for a good price.

One final note: Detail the car *after* all repairs, reconditioning, smog inspections, etc., so it looks great when potential buyers show up.

Advertising Your Car

The traditional (and unimaginative) way to advertise your car is an ad in your local newspaper. This is also the most expensive form of advertising, with results that vary greatly from one seller to the next.

For women who live alone, it may not be wise to let strangers know where you live, let alone inviting them to your house, so if you choose this method of advertising, it might be a good idea to have a male friend show the car (at his house), or pick a public place to meet—and bring your friend with you. This is especially important when it comes to a stranger road-testing your car. Some women have been assaulted in the past by men using the classifieds to find potential victims. Don't take chances—take a friend with you, instead.

If a stranger takes your car for a spin by himself, he might damage it—or steal it. Don't assume that the car he left at your place belongs to him; it could be one he "borrowed" from another seller. For women, this is a good time to bring a friend along.

Some people recommend letting potential buyers go on road-tests by themselves, reasoning that your personal sefety is more important than the money you would lose if someone damaged or stole your car. This *is* a good point, but using the "buddy system" is a lot safer than going by yourself.

Newspapers are not the only way to advertise your car. Other methods include general-purpose direct-mail advertisements (like the *Pennysaver*) and specialized ones (like *Auto Trader*) that can be found on racks at grocery and convenience stores. These are usually less expensive than advertising in major newspapers, but results vary.

Instead of print advertising, some sellers choose to display their car—with a "for sale" sign—where it will be seen by many. This can be done (for a fee, of course) on a number of car lots that display "private party" cars for sale. Not to be confused with "consignment" lots where the vehicle owner is guaranteed a set amount and the lot keeps all the money in excess of that figure, a private party car lot is simply a "physical classified ad" where potential buyers can see many cars for sale by private parties, all on one lot.

Depending on where you live or work, you may be able to display your car (for free, of course) on a vacant lot or parking lot next to a busy street. All you need is a "for sale" sign listing the price, contact phone number, and any other vital information that will fit. I used this method to sell a car for $900 more than the dealer offered as a trade-in, and it sold—for the price I was asking—the first day it was displayed.

In some areas, there may be laws against displaying your car on public streets. Also, some vacant lots and parking lots may have signs prohibiting this practice, with threats of towing away cars that ignore the warning signs, so be sure to check before trying this.

If you can't find a good location to do this for free, you might try offering to pay a service station or other business owner to let you display your car on his lot, in full view of a busy street. Even if you end up paying $10-20 to use his lot for a weekend, that's still cheaper than advertising in the newspaper. When you're negotiating, remind the lot owner that any amount is more than that space has been earning so far.

Negotiating With Buyers

How you price your car, and how you negotiate, should depend on how long you are willing to have a car for sale. The process is inconvenient and frustrating for many, so if you would like to get it over with as quickly as possible, then price your car a little lower than the competition and accept the first reasonable offer. On the other hand, if you love selling things, you may want to hold out for top dollar, but this will require greater sales ability and more advertising expenses, because it will take longer to sell your car.

Knowing your competition can be a big help in countering objections and lower offers. Check out similar cars for sale in your area to see how yours measures up, then use this information to convince potential buyers that your car is a better deal (for example, "my car has a rebuilt engine/new paint/lower mileage/new tires, etc."). Any documentation or warranties you can provide for major items is a plus, as is a written record proving that the car was properly maintained.

If you would like to learn the art of selling or negotiating, visit your local bookstore or public library and study those subjects. There have been a number of books published recently by some of the greatest salesmen and negotiators in the business.

When You've Got a Buyer

Whatever you do, don't take a personal check as payment-in-full on a car, unless you cash the check at the buyer's bank *before* giving him title and possession of the car. If a buyer insists on a same-day transaction, make him pay cash—or at least require a verified cashier's check, money order, or traveler's checks.

To avoid receiving parking tickets and other traffic violations that should be going to the new owner, make sure the title transfer is recorded immediately. Don't assume that the buyer is going to do this, because even if you send in the notice that you have sold your car, if the buyer fails to complete the title transfer, you could still end up in court trying to convince a judge that those tickets belong to someone else. Worse yet, if the buyer gets in an accident, you could be sued.

The easiest way to make sure the title transfer is recorded is to have the buyer meet you at the motor vehicle department. You bring the car, along with a completed bill of sale, the title and registration, and a current smog inspection certificate. The buyer brings the money. Give him possession of the car *after* you have the money in your hand and the necessary paperwork has been signed and turned in.

One last tip: Make sure you have included the words "this vehicle sold as is" on the bill of sale. Otherwise, if something goes wrong with the car after the sale, the buyer may claim that you gave him some kind of verbal promise that the car was in perfect condition and he would not experience any problems.

Dealer Trade-in

If you still insist on trading in your old car, in spite of the fact that you will end up with less money, get bids from several dealers before agreeing on a trade-in price. Locate the used car manager and ask if he's interested in buying your car. If he is, have him make an offer, preferably in writing. Do this at several dealers (and maybe some used car lots, too) and you will quickly learn the wholesale value of your car.

See how the dealers' bids compare to the values listed in *Edmunds Used Car Prices* or the NADA price books, then try to negotiate a better price with the highest bidders. This will be easier to do if your car is in excellent condition, because they know it will bring top dollar on their lot.

Higher bids from competitors can sometimes be used to persuade your dealer (the one who's selling you a new car) to raise his offer. However, if you've done a good job of negotiating away most of his profit on the new car, he may not be able to go much higher on your trade-in. In that case, you'll soon learn the depressing truth about how much you are getting for your old car.

CHAPTER 8

"One-Price" &
"No-Haggle" Dealers

If car dealers could create a "dream world," it would no
doubt feature an endless stream of customers who were
not only willing, but happy to pay the sticker price on new
cars—without any haggling. Of course, to make this
work, every dealer in "dream world" would charge the
same price for a particular model, eliminating [evil] competition that only forces businesses to lower their prices. To
make the dream complete, all of the sticker prices would be
high enough to guarantee that every dealer would make
more profit on every sale than they could make in a competitive environment.

Sound like a silly fantasy? Not at all! "Dream world"
has been a reality for Saturn dealers since the 1991 models
came out, and although the company hasn't been much of
a money-maker, it has succeeded in making everyone pay
retail for its cars. Other dealers have changed from skep-
tics to envious competitors, and some of them have even
tried to copy the "Saturn experience."

You've probably seen manufacturers and dealers advertising "one-price" or "no-haggle" deals on new cars. If
you're the type of person who hates the negotiating pro-

cess, a "no-haggle" deal may sound attractive, but are their prices really non-negotiable? The following sections explain the differences between "the real thing" and the copycats, and how you can take advantage of those differences to get a better deal.

Saturn: The Only True "No-Haggle" Dealer

At the present time, Saturn dealers have the only true nonnegotiable prices in the country. Every Saturn buyer pays retail (MSRP), even if he's a "shrewd negotiator," and customers seem to love it (almost as much as the dealers). How did Saturn manage to pull it off? Simple—by giving a small number of dealers exclusive territories, so they wouldn't have to compete with each other by lowering prices. Also, having a limited supply of cars helped to keep demand—and prices—high.

Saturn sales associates are trained to help customers fall in love with the car, and since there's nothing to discuss regarding price, they can focus all their talents on convincing people that the Saturn is the best small car on the market. Prospective buyers are encouraged to step on sample door panels to demonstrate their resistance to scratches and dents. (This *is* an impressive demonstration.) Design, construction, and safety features are all emphasized in a professional presentation.

The only thing missing at a Saturn dealer is sales pressure. Their sales people are paid a salary instead of commission, eliminating the pressure to "close the deal and soak the customer for as much as you can." This is all part of the "Saturn experience," designed to be the most enjoyable car buying visit anyone has ever had.

As enjoyable as this is for buyers, it's far more enjoyable for dealers—they get retail for every Saturn they sell, and the profit per car is much higher than it would be in a competitive environment. All 1995 Saturn base prices (and options) have a 13% profit margin, about twice the average profit on a similar car with a negotiable price. The following dealer cost vs. retail price information illustrates the larger profit margins on several '95 Saturn (base) models compared to several '95 Ford Escorts.

	Retail	Invoice
Saturn SL 4-Dr, 5-speed	$9995	$8696
Saturn SC2 2-Dr, auto.	$13815	$12019
Escort 3-Dr, hatchback	$9580	$8867
Escort GT 3-Dr, hatchback	$12720	$11726

As you can see, the lowest-priced Saturn model with no options or add-ons still makes a $1299 profit for the dealer, compared to a $713 profit on the lowest-priced Escort. (These profit figures do not include the 3% dealer holdback, which adds another $300 or $400 to the profit margins.) Higher-priced Saturn models, especially those with options, can generate profits exceeding $2,000 per car. No wonder Saturn dealers love their little monopoly—I mean arrangement!

The above figures also illustrate one of the major accomplishments of Saturn—getting people to (happily) pay more for cars with fixed prices than they would have to pay for similar cars with negotiable prices. Ford Escorts are similar to Saturns in size, quality, and features, but Saturns cost $500 to $1,000 more based on the retail prices—and since Escort prices are negotiable, no one has to pay retail, making the difference even greater.

So far, the success of the "Saturn experience" seems to be more the result of clever marketing and a "unique showroom atmosphere" than having a superior car. According to Consumer Reports' frequency-of-repair records, 1991 and '92 Saturns had a lot more repair problems than the newer models, but that didn't seem to have much effect on customer satisfaction; they loved the cars and "the experience" anyway.

I guess the secret to Saturn's high customer satisfaction ratings during the first two years was the illogical attitude, "I don't care if I pay more, as long as no one else pays less than I did." This attitude continues today, with many people willing to pay a premium for the enjoyable "Saturn experience." (Maybe what these consumers are really saying is that they're willing to pay $500 to $1,000 just to avoid having to deal with a salesman who's working on commission.)

The Copycats: "One-Price" & "Value-Pricing" Dealers

Saturn's success did not go unnoticed by other manufacturers and dealers, who were green with envy over the high Customer Satisfaction Index (CSI) ratings recent buyers had given the Saturn dealers—and all of those buyers paid the sticker price! After suffering for years from low CSI numbers and shrinking profit margins (due to competition), some companies and dealers are now trying to duplicate the "Saturn experience."

General Motors' "Value Pricing" programs were designed to offer substantial discounts on a number of specially-equipped models, at supposedly non-negotiable prices. To make the change to "one-price" sales, the sticker prices were lowered far below the usual MSRP. For example, a car that used to retail for a "negotiable" $20,000 might now be "value-priced" at $18,000. (In case you're worried that dealers might not be making any money at that price, that's still about $1,000 over dealer invoice, plus the 3% dealer holdback adds another $540 for a grand total of

$1,540 profit on a sale with no add-ons. It doesn't look like they'll need to apply for food stamps.)

Of course, to make the change complete, a new sales atmosphere had to be created by retraining the sales staff to treat customers in a professional, no-pressure manner. In the past, many potential car buyers felt that negotiating with a dealer was about as enjoyable as having a root canal, so dealers have set up extensive training programs to eliminate the customary high-pressure commission sales atmosphere. Salesmen at some dealers are now paid a higher salary instead of straight commission.

GM's Value Pricing dealers have been trying to convince customers that their prices are not negotiable at all, but they haven't been totally successful. Without much effort, many buyers have talked sales people into lowering prices by several hundred dollars. Others have used a car buying service to get substantial discounts off the "value price." (I guess their prices were negotiable, after all.)

The newest arrival on the "one-price/no-haggle" scene is the Oldsmobile division of General Motors. Its market share had been sinking lower and lower, and rumors had begun to spread throughout the industry that the division was going to be eliminated. GM repeatedly said that it remained committed to the Oldsmobile line, but the rumors persisted. Some consumers may have been afraid to buy a car that might be discontinued, and average sales per Olds dealer fell to 100-150 cars per year (compared to 400-800 for a number of other dealers).

Oldsmobile General Manager John Rock decided that the cure for slumping sales was to pattern the division after Saturn. The goal was to have a one-price/no-haggle, no pressure, pleasant car-buying environment—known as the "Straightforward Approach" with "Simplified Pricing"—where every buyer would (gladly) pay retail. However, Rock's plan has two big holes in it. First, Saturn can get away with their no-haggle prices because there are so few Saturn dealers that they have a virtual monopoly, but there are too many Olds dealers in the country to stop them from cutting prices to compete. Second, the Olds dealers seem to be divided on their support for the new program—some like it, and some complain loudly by writing open letters in trade publications.

For example, one Olds dealer who supports the new program said they were making over $1,600 gross profit per car, while another dealer complained that their new-car profit has dropped $200 per unit. (If those two dealers were *averaging* $1,600 to $1,800 profit per car under the old "start at sticker and dicker" plan, they either had a lot of unsophisticated buyers who paid too much, or they made $3,000 to $4,000 per car from a few "pigeons" to make up for the rest.)

Some Olds dealers said they were behind the no-haggle program, but they needed more margin to use with customers who still wanted to negotiate! They also said they could use more margin for customers who are "upside-down" (they owe more on their car than it's worth) or need more for their trade-in. Apparently, not everyone is embracing the new program.

Other manufacturers have offered "one-price" deals to increase sales on certain slow-moving models, but these weren't really non-negotiable prices. For example, some Ford Escorts and Thunderbirds were supposed to have "reduced, no-haggle prices," but many dealers cut prices even lower to sell more cars.

Making the transition to "one-price" from "start at sticker and dicker" is proving to be a tough sell after decades of doing business the old way. When customers are told how the new "professional, dignified, one-price program" works, many buyers have expressed disbelief—"Sure, I understand how it works. Now, let's talk discount!"

Buyers may be wise to not believe statements that everyone will pay the same price for a particular car. A 1992 study of two dozen dealers who switched to "one-price" selling revealed that one-third of them changed their prices when factory incentives went up or down. Others in the study "adjusted" their prices when inventory levels changed, and some changed their prices weekly or even daily. So, if it's going to bother you that someone else may pay less than you for the same car, then make sure you get the best deal possible—not necessarily the first one mentioned.

How to Buy a "Value-Priced" Car for Less

For those who hate the new-car negotiating process, a specially-equipped "value-priced" deal is a lot better than paying close to retail under the old system. However, if you want to buy one of these cars and get an even better deal, assume that everything is negotiable and make a written offer for a lower price. Even though the salesman claims that their prices are not negotiable, insist that he write up your (lower) offer and present it to the manager—and remind him that if they turn it down, you'll make the same offer at all of their competitors. (See Chapter 11 for the whole negotiating process.) Better yet, just use the Car-Bargains car buying service.

What Car Dealers Don't Want You to Know

CHAPTER 9

Timing is Everything: When to Buy

When it comes to getting the lowest price on a new car, timing is everything. If you're in the right place at the right time, you can get a great deal; show up too early or too late, and you'll pay too much.

Buying Too Soon

The new car market is a perfect illustration for the law of supply and demand: whenever a dealer has more buyers than cars, everyone pays retail (or more). Two recent examples of this were the Mazda Miata and the Dodge Viper, both arriving with much publicity and little inventory. The initial buyers of those cars wanted them so bad that many people paid $5,000 (or more) over sticker, just to be the first one on their block with that particular car. In the case of the Miata, thousands more became available within a year, and anyone could eventually buy one for sticker or less.

Automakers will hate me for saying this, but my best advice for car buyers is to avoid the initial introduction of any new model. First, new models almost always have more problems than models that have been out for a while. (So let them work the bugs out on someone else's car.) Second, you'll rarely be offered any kind of rebate or discounted price during the first few months of a new model introduction because the supply of cars is usually rather limited.

Later in the year, however, discounts often become available as the supply increases, and if the new model isn't selling very well, the factory may come out with rebates and other incentives. (This sometimes happens within 2 to 3 months if the factory was too optimistic in estimating sales.)

Factory Rebates & Incentives

Factory rebates and other incentives are just disguised price cuts that are used to increase sales when things get slow. Automakers hate to use rebates because they cut into their profits, but since buyers seem to stay away when no rebates are offered, it looks like they're saying that the cars are overpriced. So dealers cut their prices (with rebates) and buyers return to the showrooms.

Buyers need to use a service like Fighting Chance® (see Chapter 10) to find out what incentives are available and when they expire. Incentive programs come and go, so if they don't have one right now on the car you want, it might be worth it to wait a month or two in case one comes along. (Don't bother waiting if you're trying to buy a real hot-selling model — they don't offer incentives on those.)

Some dealer incentives are based on volume, which means that the more cars they sell, the higher the incentive amount on every car sold during the program. *This type of incentive can give a dealer a good reason to sell you a car at a little-or-no profit price*, because one more sale could end up generating thousands of extra incentive dollars for the dealership. The best time to buy a car that has a volume incentive is right before the program ends, within the last few days.

Sales Goals, Quotas, & Little-or-No Profit Deals

Before a salesman will consider selling a car for little-or-no profit, he has to have a real good reason, and that's where sales goals come into play. Most salesmen work on commission and will be affected by some type of a *monthly* goal or quota. The benefits of meeting a sales goal can range anywhere from keeping his job to winning an expensive vacation trip, or getting paid a higher percentage on all the cars he sold during that month. Obviously, if your sale is the one that "puts him over the top," he will benefit greatly even though the deal has little-or-no profit in it for the dealership.

The whole sales department may also have monthly goals that could encourage the sales manager to approve several low-profit deals at the end of the month in order to make the final numbers higher. And since most incentive programs also expire around the end of the month, the last few days of the month are often a good time to get the lowest price on a car. (Just be sure to check the expiration dates of any incentive programs before deciding when to buy.)

Year-End Clearance Sales: Buying Last Year's Model

Some car buyers like to wait until the new models arrive, then they purchase last year's model during a dealer's "big year-end sale." While it is true that they are getting a "brand new car" at a reduced price, they're also buying a car that is already one year old and has probably depreciated several thousand dollars before they even get to drive it home. If that fact doesn't bother you, and you still prefer to buy last year's model, there are a few things you should know before buying one.

The best year-end deals can usually be found on cars that have a manufacturer's "carryover allowance," an incentive the dealer receives for every previous year model vehicle left on his lot when the new models come out. (Why do they do this? Because the automakers know that a dealer who has a lot of cars left over will not order as many new models as he would if his lot was empty.) GM and Ford usually have carryover allowances based on 5% of the MSRP (sticker) on all models every year, although sometimes they may leave out their hottest-selling cars. Some imports have a specific dollar amount, which could be as much as $6,000 to $10,000 on a luxury car.

Here's an example of how a carryover can affect the actual dealer's cost on a domestic car: On a typical $20,000 (retail) car, the dealer would get back an additional $1,000 (carryover) along with the usual holdback ($600 at 3%) and any factory-to-dealer incentives (we'll use $1,000), adding up to $2,600 off the dealer's cost. (Don't forget—none of this will show up on the factory invoice.) Subtract the $2,600 from the typical factory invoice of $17,000 on our $20,000 car, and you'll see that the dealer's actual cost is now only $14,400.

Now the dealer may not be willing to sell the car at his cost, but keep in mind that it is last year's model—and he's paying the bank interest on the car for as long as it sits on his lot—so, if he can't find another buyer at that price, he'll be forced to sell it below cost. Offer to buy it for his actual cost ($14,400 in our example) and see what happens. If that doesn't work, offer to let him keep some (or all) of the holdback money (which means raising your offer to about $14,700 or $15,000). Don't go much higher, or you'll end up paying more than the car is worth. Remember—it's already a year old, so it's depreciated several thousand dollars, and it was only "worth" a little more than $17,000 when it was new (because that's the price a shrewd buyer would have paid).

As you can see, there is the possibility of huge discounts on year-end models, so make sure you receive them if you plan on buying a car this way. Don't settle for less, or you'll end up losing a lot of money if you sell the car or trade it in within several years.

The Law of Supply and Demand: Use It to Your Advantage

How the law of supply and demand affects the sale of cars is fairly simple: 1) when there are more buyers than cars, prices go up, and 2) when there are more cars than buyers, prices go down. The secret to getting the best deal is to only buy during the second market condition. As long as you don't have to buy that car immediately, you can always wait until the market favors you rather than the dealer. Also, by shopping around and making dealers compete for your business, you're helping to create favorable market conditions for yourself.

Here's how to tip the scales in your favor: go to buy a car when few buyers are around. How do you do that? Simple—go at times that others avoid. The busiest days at car dealers are usually Saturday, Sunday, during big advertised sales, and when the weather is nice. Instead, go on a weekday, around holidays like Christmas and Easter, whenever the weather is bad, and if you really want to see empty showrooms, go during the Superbowl. [I know, you don't want one that bad.]

CHAPTER 10

Homework for Car Buyers

Emotional and impulsive shoppers always end up with the worst deals, so avoid that trap by taking the time to become a cool, calm, educated buyer. Decide ahead of time that the purpose of your first dealer visit will be *to look at everything and buy nothing.* Don't bring your checkbook or the title to your car, and don't agree to buy anything—no matter how good it looks or sounds.

When you are visiting dealerships, salesmen will swarm around you even though you tell them you're "just looking." Tell them you're not going to buy anything for three or four weeks and they'll usually disappear so you can enjoy looking at different models. Take your time; look at everything that interests you. Collect brochures and other information, and don't be afraid to ask questions. Then go home—in your old car.

After visiting several dealers to see what kinds of cars you like (and can afford), the next step is to research those models to see what kind of ratings they have, and also to see if those models have any "twins or cousins" that are less expensive. When you've narrowed the field down to one or two models, and you've done all your research, then you're ready to set a target price and make an offer. (Setting a target price and making an offer are both covered in Chapter 11.)

The following sections cover various categories that should be considered before deciding which car to buy. A resource section is also included (at the end) to help you find the information you need, from ratings to "twins" to actual dealer cost, even the name of the best car buying service I've found.

Safety

Safety is always ranked by consumers as an important feature on a new car, but how can people tell which cars are safer than others? All new cars don't offer the same crash protection, and some don't have 4-wheel anti-lock brakes and/or dual air bags. Fortunately, there are several groups who provide safety ratings for all the new cars every year.

Reliability/Quality

There are significant differences in quality from one car to the next, so don't assume that your car is going to be trouble-free just because it's new. Choosing a car with a good repair history can help you save money in two ways: 1) in general, cars with good reliability/quality ratings usually have lower overall repair costs, and 2) if you're going to buy an extended warranty, the price of the warranty will be lower.

Checking the repair history of a particular model before purchasing becomes even more important in the case of a used car. Expensive repairs are most likely to occur after a car is six or seven years old, and most used cars are sold without any kind of warranty, so choosing the wrong car can turn out to be an expensive mistake. In looking up repair histories in *Consumer Reports*, one issue will usually go back only eight years, so if you're considering a car that's more than eight years old, just go to the library and ask for an older (April) issue that would have the year models you want.

Fuel Economy

Unfortunately, the cars with the best fuel economy ratings are usually the smallest (and lightest) models, which means they won't do very well in an accident with a larger car. [Sorry, that's physics.] Also, the most miserly vehicles are usually the ones with the smallest engines and the fewest luxury features (like air conditioning). For most people, fuel economy will end up being a compromise, settling for less mileage, but more safety, power, and/or accessories.

Insurance Cost

This item is frequently overlooked until after the new car is driven home. Of course, by that time it's too late to pick another car because the insurance is going to cost too much. Rates can vary dramatically from one model to another, so be sure to call your agent for a quote *before* you make the final decision. And don't assume you'll automatically be covered when you buy a new car—let your agent know in advance when you plan on taking delivery of your new car.

A warning for new lease customers: leases usually require higher liability coverage (100/300) than you may normally carry, so don't decide to lease at the last minute without finding out what the insurance costs are going to be. In states that have high insurance rates, this requirement can significantly increase the cost of driving a new car every two or three years.

Value/Depreciation

Buyers who plan on replacing their cars every 3-5 years should also consider the future resale value when deciding which car to buy. Some models can lose as much as 72% of their value (starting from MSRP) in the first 48 months, while others may only drop 46%. Choosing a model with poor resale value can easily add thousands to the cost of driving a car.

One good way to limit resale losses is to buy for as much below MSRP as possible. *Don't forget—a car won't be worth any more money four years from now just because you paid too much for it when it was new.*

Of course, if you plan on keeping the car forever, future market value may not be a major consideration. Just keep in mind that a model may have poor resale value because it has a history of needing more repairs.

"Orphans"

One thing a lot of car buyers don't consider is the possibility that their new car may become an "orphan" when the automaker (or dealer) quits or goes out of business. None of the major companies (GM, Ford, Chrysler, Honda, Toyota, Nissan) seem to be in any danger, but there are a number of smaller companies—and newcomers—whose continued presence in the U.S. market is not necessarily a sure thing.

In the past four years, automakers Daihatsu, Peugeot, and Sterling all decided to quit selling cars in this country, and Yugo went bankrupt. The unfortunate owners of those cars now have trouble getting parts and service (because those dealer networks have dried up), and their cars have dropped in value. To prevent that from happening to you, be sure to check out the financial strength—and commitment to the U.S. market—of any smaller automaker you are considering.

Financing

You can usually save money by arranging your own financing, so call your credit union or bank, shop around at other lenders, and find out if any below-market factory financing is available. Get your loan pre-approved at the best rate you can find—outside the dealership—and do this *before* you begin negotiating on a car. (See Chapter 6 for details on figuring out whether to take a rebate or use the low-APR factory financing.)

Extended Warranties

Don't wait until you're in the dealer's finance office to decide whether to get an extended warranty or not—if you do, chances are you'll pay far more than the coverage is worth. Shop around to find the best deal on a warranty *before* you go to a dealer to make an offer on a car. (See Chapter 5 for information on extended warranties and where to buy them at discount prices.)

Dealer Invoice & Incentives

To get the best deal on a new car, you have to know the dealer's cost so you can figure out how much to offer. And knowing "factory invoice" or "dealer invoice" isn't good enough—you also need current information on any factory-to-dealer incentives, allowances, and holdback money. The best sources for this information are listed at the end of this section. (Be sure to read Chapter 2, "The Truth About Dealer Cost.")

Leasing

The worst leasing deals are usually the ones salesmen try to talk people into, the ones they offer to the average buyer. To get a "good lease"—if there is such a thing—you have to write your own. So, if you insist on using this method of financing to drive a new car, make sure you learn how it works, or you'll end up paying too much. (See Chapter 1 for a lesson on leasing.)

Using a Car Buying Service

For those who hate the whole negotiating process and would normally pay "sticker" just to avoid a confrontation, I recommend using the CarBargains buying service. In fact, they're so sure they can get a better price than you can, they guarantee it—or your money back. And they can tell you where to get the best prices on factory-sponsored service contracts. (See Chapter 12 for details.)

RESOURCES

Published Ratings

Consumer Reports, Annual Auto Issue (April)
****Most comprehensive data on frequency-of-repairs
****Used car reliability reports
    New car facts, safety & reliability ratings

The Car Book, by Jack Gillis
****Most comprehensive safety data & ratings
    Other ratings: fuel economy, maintenance costs,
                    warranties, tires
    New car facts, EPA mileage figures & much more

Books: Retail & Dealer Invoice Prices

1) *Edmund's New Car Prices*
2) *Pace Buyer's Guides, New Car Prices*
(available in most bookstores)

Books: Used Car Prices

1) *Edmund's Used Car Prices*
2) *Kelley Blue Book/Used Car Guide, Consumer Edition*
(available in most bookstores)

Services: Dealer Cost & Incentive Information

FIGHTING CHANCE®
5318 East 2nd St., #242
Long Beach, CA 90803
(310) 433-8489
(800) 288-1134

****Four stars! Best information service I've found.
Tells you dealer invoice on model of your choice
plus a *CarDeals* report: dealer incentives on all cars.
Provides pricing info on all trim levels of the model
you select w/o additional charge. One fee includes
current & previous year model, as well as actual
prices other buyers have paid for the same model.
Will also help customers examine lease figures.
Cost: 1st car $19.95, $7 for each additional car.

Consumer Reports 1-800-AUTO-INFO™

Provides dealer invoice and incentive information.
Basic info for a low price: $12 for the 1st car, $10

for each additional car. (This can quickly add up— if you want prices on all 3 trim levels for the Dodge Caravan, you have to pay $32.) Can provide safety and reliability report for up to 3 cars for $12 (does not include new car prices—that's extra).

CarBargains Car Buying Service

CarBargains
733 15th Street NW, Ste. 820
Washington, DC 20005
(202) 347-9612
(800) 475-7283

****Four stars! CarBargains is the best car buying service I've found. Cost: $150. Guaranteed to get a lower price than you can on your own, or your money back. Can also provide buyers with names of dealers promising to sell factory-sponsored service contracts for less than $50 over cost.

Leasing Guides/Software

CHART Software
152 Woodcreek Drive, N.
Safety Harbor, FL 34695
(813) 791-4955
(800) 418-8450

CHART distributes 3 leasing products:
    1) *Automotive Lease Guide* contains retail and residual values used in determining lease payments for new & used cars. Cost: $12.50

2) "Expert Lease" software will perform lease/buy analysis, calculate lease payments, determine APR of lease, determine dealer margin, and analyze single-payment leases. Used by accountants and other financial advisors. Take your laptop computer to the dealer to analyze their leasing deals! Recommended by *Money Magazine, Kiplinger's Personal Finance Magazine*, and many others. (IBM compatible only) Cost: $59.95

3) "Expert Lease Pro" contains all the features of Expert Lease, plus the following: retail and invoice prices for new cars & trucks, *Automotive Lease Guide* residual values for all new vehicles, CarDeals report on all dealer incentives, one free update of software and data. (IBM compatible only) Cost: $99.95

"Twins & Cousins"

"Twins & cousins" are similar models sold under different names. These cars often have the same basic body style, engine, and drivetrain. In most cases, the only differences are in trim (style) and levels of luxury, but there can be significant differences in price, so you may be able to save money by purchasing the less expensive twin. The following list contains the "twins & cousins" for the 1995 model year:

CHRYSLER CORPORATION
Chrysler Cirrus/Dodge Stratus
Chrysler Concorde/Dodge Intrepid/Eagle Vision
Chrysler LHS/New Yorker
Chrysler Sebring/Dodge Avenger/Mitsubishi Galant
Chrysler Town & Country/Dodge Grand Caravan/
         Plymouth Voyager

Dodge Caravan/Plymouth Voyager
Dodge Spirit/Plymouth Acclaim
Dodge Stealth/Mitsubishi 3000 GT
Eagle Summit/Mitsubishi Mirage
Eagle Talon/Mitsubishi Eclipse

FORD MOTOR COMPANY
Ford Contour/Mercury Mystique
Ford Crown Victoria/Lincoln Town Car/
      Mercury Grand Marquis
Ford Escort/Mercury Tracer
Ford Explorer/Mazda Navajo
Ford Probe/Mazda MX-6
Ford Taurus/Mercury Sable
Ford Thunderbird/Lincoln Mark VIII/Mercury Cougar
Mercury Villager/Nissan Quest

GENERAL MOTORS
Buick Century/Oldsmobile Cutlass Ciera
Buick LeSabre/Olds 88/Pontiac Bonneville
Buick Park Avenue/Olds 98
Buick Regal/Olds Cutlass Supreme/Pontiac Grand Prix
Buick Riviera/Olds Aurora
Buick Skylark/Olds Achieva/Pontiac Grand Am
Buick Roadmaster/Chevrolet Caprice
Chevrolet Astro/GMC Safari
Chevrolet Blazer/Olds Bravada/GMC Jimmy
Chevrolet Camaro/Pontiac Firebird
Chevrolet Cavalier/Pontiac Sunfire
Chevrolet Corsica/Beretta
Chevrolet Lumina/Monte Carlo
Chevrolet Lumina Minivan/Olds Silhouette/
      Pontiac Trans Sport
Chevrolet S10 Pickup/GMC Sonoma
Geo Metro/Suzuki Swift

Geo Prizm/Toyota Corolla
Geo Tracker/Suzuki Sidekick

HONDA
Honda Passport/Isuzu Rodeo

TOYOTA
Toyota Camry/Lexus ES 300

CHAPTER 11

How to Negotiate

If you skipped the first part of the book, you need to go back—this chapter is only for knowledgeable buyers who have done their homework and understand the business. By this time, you should know all about true dealer's cost and the numerous tricks salesmen use to get more of your money. You've thoroughly researched the model you want, including its mechanical and safety track records, you have a pre-approved car loan from the lender of your choice, and you've figured out a low-profit target price.

Before you start negotiating in person, there's a great strategy that's worth trying: "bidding by mail." The lowest bid can then be used to negotiate a better price with another dealer, or if it's the best deal you can find, use it to buy your new car or truck.

Bidding by Mail (or Fax)

In "bidding by mail," you get a number of dealers to make blind bids on a new car, without you being there. This has two big advantages: 1) they know that you will buy somewhere else if their bid isn't the lowest, and 2) since you're not there, they can't use any of their tricks to get more money out of you.

Make a list of all the dealers you would be willing to buy from, then call them on the phone to get the names of their fleet managers along with their mailing addresses (or fax numbers). If a dealer doesn't have a fleet manager, get the name of the sales manager instead.

Draft a convincing letter to be sent to all the fleet managers on your list. The letters should be identical with the exception of the manager/dealer identification, and they must communicate that you are a serious and knowledgeable buyer.

In the letter, state that you are going to buy a specific model new vehicle, listing the color and any options, then ask them to quote you their best price. Mention that you are also getting quotes from other dealers in your area and the one with the lowest quote gets your business. Also mention that you have a pre-approved loan, but would be willing to consider any special factory financing that may be available.

Let them know you're aware of the dealer invoice and any factory-to-dealer incentives, so you expect the most competitive bids to be far below MSRP. Remind them to leave the customer rebate money (if applicable) out of their quotes; that money belongs to the buyer, so don't let the dealers use it to make their bids look better than they really are.

Be sure to mention that you do not want anything added to the car that's not factory-installed, especially paint sealer, fabric protection, undercoating, alarm system, etc. (Optional: If they can provide you with a factory-backed extended warranty at a *reasonable* price, you may be interested.) Ask them to include and itemize all charges in their quotes.

Your letter should have your name and address, both home and work phone numbers, and a fax number if you have one. Close with the statement that you will be making a final decision in two weeks, so you will assume that dealers who fail to respond by then are not interested. Thank them in advance, sign your name, mail the letters, and wait for a response! (If you can fax the letters instead of mailing them, this whole process may only take one week.)

Some dealers won't respond to this approach because they would rather have the "home court advantage," so be sure to send out at least four or five letters. If any of the managers try to get you to come in before quoting a firm price, tell them you're not interested in doing business that way.

Negotiating in Person

Your overall negotiating strategy is to appear to be a serious, well-informed, unemotional buyer who has no preference for one dealer over another when it comes to purchasing a new car. If a salesman can tell that you're hopelessly in love with a car on his lot—or that you have some reason for not doing business with his competitors—you won't get the best possible deal, so find a way to conceal those emotions.

When you're ready to start negotiating, pick *at least* two or three dealerships you will give initial offers to, then gather your car information (vehicle worksheet, dealer invoice and incentive figures, etc.) to take with you. Your goal is to deal directly with a manager, so you can get a "house sale" without any commission being paid to a salesman.

Call ahead to make an appointment; try to meet with the fleet manager first, but if they won't let you, ask for the sales manager instead. Should they refuse to let you deal with a manager, tell them you are going to buy a car somewhere else, then call the next dealer on your list. Only deal with a salesman as a last resort—since his commission is a percentage of the profit, he normally won't be interested in a low-profit sale.

Tell the manager/salesman you have decided which car to buy and you are prepared to make an offer. Refuse to discuss any trade-in at this time. When he asks how you are going to pay for the car, tell him you have a pre-approved loan, but you are open to other financing options. Don't give him your driver's license or Social Security number, unless you want him to run a quick credit check. (They do that so they'll know how much of a monthly payment you can afford, then they'll try every trick in the book to charge you as much as you can afford.) Don't fall for it; just tell them it isn't necessary—your credit is good.

Don't show all your cards at once; if you tell him up front that you know all their tricks so he's not going to be able to rip you off, you'll probably make him so mad that you'll never be able to buy a car from him at a reasonable price. Let him think he has the advantage, even though the advantage will be yours if you know the dealer's cost and their tricks. If he thinks they might finance your new car, you may get a better price, so tell him you'll be willing to discuss financing *after* you've agreed on price.

Use the same strategy for any trade-in—tell him you'll discuss it afterwards, but count on selling your old car yourself, knowing that a dealer is not going to pay more than wholesale (if that much) unless he's made a fortune on your new car.

Whatever you do, don't give them your old car keys or a "good faith" deposit before you've agreed on a price. An unscrupulous dealer will just use these to hold you hostage while they try to wear you down, claiming that someone has misplaced them so you can't leave. A deposit is only necessary *after* your offer is accepted and you have a written contract signed by the manager.

Your Initial Offer

Your initial offer should be high enough to contain a minimal profit for the dealer—if it doesn't, they'll think that you have no idea what their cost is and your bid was just a wild guess. Make a written offer to purchase at the dealer invoice price *minus* any other factory-to-dealer incentives. Let the dealer keep the holdback money as his profit.

The following example would leave $630 profit for the dealer, assuming a 3% holdback, $1,000 factory-to-dealer incentive, and a purchase price of $17,500.

Vehicle w/options MSRP	$21,000
Dealer invoice	$18,500
Minus dealer incentive	-1,000
Your initial offer	$17,500

You should try to get most of the incentive money if there's a factory-to-dealer cash incentive involved, which means you'll be buying for hundreds (or thousands) of dollars below the dealer invoice. Settle for half of the incentive money *later*, if that's the best you can do.

Depending on the MSRP and the holdback percentage, the dealer's profit on your initial offer would be roughly $350-700. They would love to make more, but some dealers will take a low-profit deal like this. After all, a low-profit deal is better than no deal at all. (Even a no-profit deal could end up making them money —on other cars they sell—if the car is part of a volume-based incentive plan.)

After you've presented your initial offer, the manager/

salesman will probably say that they couldn't possibly sell the car for that price because it's below their cost. (If you are dealing with a salesman, he may not know what the dealer's cost is.) Now is the time to pull out your printout from Fighting Chance® (or Consumer Reports) and show him that you know exactly what their cost is: less than the amount of your offer.

When you do this, don't have a smirk on your face or a cocky attitude, just calmly show him what the dealer's cost is, including the holdback and any factory incentives. Be prepared for him to challenge the numbers—when he does, calmly suggest that he get the dealer invoice to see if the numbers are correct, but don't expect him to show it to you. Insist that your offer be presented to management.

If the person you're dealing with says he has to present the offer to his boss, tell him that you have another appointment so you can only wait ten minutes for him to return with an answer. Also tell him that is your best offer for that day, and if your offer is rejected, you will be leaving immediately to make the same offer at three or four other dealers. Then wait for their response—but only for ten minutes. When their time is up, leave the dealership.

Unless it's your lucky day, they probably won't accept your initial offer without your walking out first. (That's OK, it's all part of the plan.) Every time one of your offers is rejected, tell them to give you a signed, written quote of the lowest price they would take, then walk out.

When you have their counteroffer (or their ten minutes are up because they're stalling), leave the dealership immediately and repeat the process at the next dealer on your list. Continue making the same initial offer until one of the dealers agrees to sell at your price or you've run out of dealers. Do not—under any circumstances—increase your initial offer on the first day until you've presented it to all of the dealers on your list.

Incidentally, if anyone refuses to negotiate on your terms (including a refusal to quote you their "best price"), tell them you're sure you can find a dealer who will, then thank them for their time and leave. Be polite, because you want them to change their mind and call you back.

Your Best Weapon: Walking Out

Remember that your best negotiating weapon is your ability (and willingness) to walk out after a dealer rejects your offer, instead of staying to negotiate further. If you don't walk out, the salesman will assume that he hasn't heard your best offer yet, so he won't accept a low bid.

You will usually have to make at least two offers at the same dealership before you get a good deal, and you'll have to walk out after they turn down each of your offers to convince them that they're not going to get any more money out of you. Yes, this takes a few visits to the same dealer, but if each visit is a polite "take-it-or-leave-it" offer (instead of a two or three hour battle with a salesman), it won't take that much time. *This is the only way to get the best deal on a car.*

What usually happens when you walk out (after they reject your offer) is that they will eventually run after you, often waiting until you're back in your car to see if you're bluffing. To get you back inside, they'll say anything. ("Mr. Smith, let me present your offer to my boss one more time. Since it's the end of the day, I'm sure he will accept it.") They won't let you get away if they know you're a serious buyer; their goal is to get you back inside so they can sell you a car—for more money.

When they try this, tell them you're not going back inside unless they're ready to accept your offer. If necessary, give them your phone number and tell them to call you when they're serious about selling the car. Remind them that you are going to several other dealers to make the same offer, then leave.

Your Revised Target Price

Assuming that none of your initial offers were accepted, you should now have a number of bids (written counteroffers) from the dealers you visited. The next step is to figure out a new target price for your second written offer, one that will be harder for dealers to reject.

Your new offering price should be about $200 to $300 more than your original offer. On lower-priced cars (with an MSRP of $9,000 to $12,000), an additional $200 is a substantial increase that should be tempting to some dealers, since those vehicles have a lower profit margin to begin with. On mid-sized (and larger) cars, you might have to increase your original offer by $250 to $300 to make it attractive.

If there is a factory-to-dealer incentive, your new target price could still be hundreds (or thousands) below dealer invoice; if no dealer incentive exists, your new bid may be 1-2% over invoice. *Do not offer more than 2% over dealer invoice on your second bid.*

Before you present your second offer, go over the written counteroffers you received. Wait until at least four or five days have gone by since your initial offer, then phone all of the dealers on your list and ask if they've reconsidered your offer. Tell the dealers with the higher bids what the low bid was, then ask if they will beat that bid to sell you the car. They probably won't offer to beat it by more than a token amount (maybe as little as $25 or $50), but that's OK because you're not going to offer that much (unless a new bid is so close to your revised target price that you're willing to accept it). *Don't make any commitments at this time*—tell them you'll think it over and call them back when you're ready.

Use the information gained from the phone calls to "fine-tune" your new target price. If you get several bids that are close to your new target price, lower it. For example, if several dealers say they'll sell for $400 more than your initial offer, you know you're getting close to a figure that will be tempting, so only increase your offering price $200 (instead of $300).

Your Second Offer

Present the second offer in the same manner as the first, asking for a written counteroffer if your offer is rejected. Remind them that you will be making the same offer at several other dealers, then leave. Don't let them talk you into raising your offer during that visit—there's a much better chance that they'll compromise first if you walk out after they reject your offer. Be sure to present your second offer to all of the dealers on your list before you consider increasing your bid (unless one of them accepts your offer, in which case you're done).

As you start offering dealers $500 to $800 over dealer's true cost—*not invoice*—some of them will worry that one of the others might accept your offer if they turn you down, so don't be too quick to raise your second offer until a week has gone by and you don't have any takers. If that happens, call the dealers back and ask if they've reconsidered your offer.

Unless you're in a seller's market (which is rare), you should be able to find a dealer who's tempted by one of your offers. In a seller's market, when dealers are able to sell all the cars they want without slashing prices, you may end up paying 3% to 4% over dealer's invoice—especially if you're not willing to wait several months for another incentive program to come along.

129

If you make it through your whole dealer list with two offers, resulting in no deals or good counteroffers, you might want to consider using CarBargains' car buying service. This is especially true if your second offer was 2% over dealer invoice. (In 1994, CarBargains got dealer bids that were *below invoice* for 40% of their customers. See Chapter 12 for more information.)

Should you decide against using a buying service after your second offers are rejected, raise your offering price by $200 (or $100 to $150 on lower-priced cars) and repeat the process. If your new price is now around 4% over dealer invoice and you can't find any takers, you may want to reevaluate the timing of your offers—it might be worthwhile to wait a month or two until incentives change or one of the dealers is more motivated to sell. *Paying much more than 4% over invoice is not a bargain on most cars.*

The "Little-or-No Profit Deal"

For those shrewd negotiators (and thrifty shoppers) who want to buy a new car for the absolute, rock-bottom, lowest price anyone will ever get, and don't care how many visits or how much time it takes to get what they want, here's how to negotiate a "little-or-no profit deal" on a new car. Keep in mind that this is not easy to do and your success will depend on persistence, timing, luck, and finding a desperate salesman or dealer. Only a small percentage of buyers will be able to pull this off.

Use the negotiating process outlined in this chapter, but start with a target price that contains no profit for the dealer. This means that you will start with the dealer invoice price, then subtract all factory-to-dealer incentives and holdback money to arrive at "true dealer cost" for that vehicle. Your target price could be hundreds or thousands below dealer invoice, depending on the amount of dealer incentive. (Accurate information on dealer cost is crucial when using this strategy, so be sure to use Fighting Chance® or Consumer Reports for invoice and incentive information. See Chapter 10.)

The following example shows how far below MSRP a "no-profit" bid can be. Dealer holdback is 3% of the list price and there is a $1,000 factory-to-dealer incentive.

Vehicle w/options MSRP $21,000	
Dealer invoice	$18,500
Minus dealer holdback	-630
Minus dealer incentive	-1,000
Your initial offer	$16,870

Timing is the key ingredient of this strategy—you must present your "no-profit" bid to the right person at the right time. An offer like this that helps a salesman or manager meet a quota (or win a contest) may be tempting if it's presented at the end of the month, because quotas and contests are often based on monthly sales. A no-profit sale on a vehicle that's part of a volume-based factory-to-dealer incentive program can generate considerable profits for a dealer, so present these offers at the end of the incentive program.

Present your "no-profit" bid to as many dealers as you can until your offer is accepted or you run out of dealers. Be sure to walk out after each bid is rejected, and don't increase your offering price until after your bid is presented and rejected by all of the dealers on your list.

If you have to raise your bid after the first round because all of the dealers rejected it, only increase your offer by $200 for the second round, making it a "$200 profit" deal.

The "Year-end Clearance Sale"

Should you decide to visit one of those big year-end clearance sales to find a "great deal" on a brand new car that's now last year's model, be sure to use the "little-or-no profit" strategy when making an offer. Even though these cars have no miles on them, they're still one year old and depreciation has reduced their market value by at least 20%. Try not to pay much more than the dealer's true cost on one of these vehicles, because the car may not even be worth that much.

The following example includes a 3% dealer holdback based on MSRP and a 5% dealer (carryover) incentive because the car is left over from last year. Notice that the dealer's true cost (your initial offer) is slighter higher than the estimated market value of the vehicle.

Vehicle w/options MSRP	$20,000
Dealer invoice	$18,000
Minus dealer holdback	-600
Minus carryover	-1,000
Your initial offer	$16,400

$$\$20,000 - \$4,000 = \$16,000$$
$$(\text{MSRP} - 20\% \text{ dep.} = \text{market value})$$

When You've Got a Deal

When you've reached an agreement on price, they'll want to discuss financing, trade-in, and the usual array of "after-sell" rip-offs designed to increase the dealer's profit margin. If you've done your homework, and you stand your ground, they won't be able to take advantage of you.

(This means you'll probably use your own lender, sell your own car, and refuse to pay for anything other than tax, license, and destination charge.)

Charges You Don't Have to Pay

Some common unnecessary, overpriced, and/or worthless "second sticker" items added on by dealers include: fabric protection, paint sealer, rustproofing/under-coating, pin-striping, car alarms, "special value package," "protection package," floor mats, etc. These are just "cash cows" for the dealer— don't pay for any of them.

If they claim that you have to pay for one or more items on the "second sticker" because they're already on the car, tell them to take those items off or get you another car without them. Just say that you don't want those things on your car and you're not going to pay for them. Let them know you'll cancel the purchase if they insist on charging you for unwanted "options." (See Chapter 3.)

Beware of charges for "dealer prep" and "national advertising"—don't pay them. Dealers are paid by the manufacturer for dealer preparation, so if you pay for it, they get paid twice. (This is obviously a very profitable rip-off, often adding about $200 to the dealer's pocket.) Advertising is a normal business expense that should not be added to a customer's final bill. (This rip-off is usually priced at 1% of the MSRP.)

Watch for items listed as "processing charges" or "closing costs." What they're trying to do is make you pay for their employees handling the paperwork, a normal cost of doing business. A $10 or $20 fee may not be worth fighting over, but watch out for a $100 (or more) paperwork processing charge—don't pay it.

If the dealer is handling the financing, he will probably try to sell you credit life or disability insurance. Don't fall for this—if you really need it (and you probably don't) you can always buy it from your own insurance agent for a lot less.

Everyone who buys a car will be told by the finance and insurance "specialist" that they should buy an extended warranty to protect themselves from expensive repair bills after the original warranty runs out. These high-profit warranties are always good for the dealer's bottom line, but not always good for the buyer; sometimes they are an absolute rip-off. Before you decide whether to buy an extended warranty or not, be sure to read Chapter 5.

Charges You Do Have to Pay

The list of items you do have to pay for is fairly short: the destination/freight charge, sales tax, license fees, and the car itself.

One Last Note

Before you take delivery of your new car (or sign papers acknowledging delivery), be sure to give it a thorough inspection. You'll have a much better chance of getting things fixed to your satisfaction before you actually take delivery. (See Chapter 14.)

CHAPTER 12

CarBargains:
A Shortcut to Savings

Some people just don't have the ability (or the desire) to do battle with car dealers, so arming them with industry secrets is not going to save them any money when they buy a new car. So, should these people just resign themselves to paying hundreds or thousands more than someone else for the same car or truck? Absolutely not—they should use CarBargains!

Why I Recommend CarBargains

CarBargains is a service provided by the Center for the Study of Services, a non-profit consumer group in Washington, D.C. Unlike auto brokers and other car buying services that are "for-profit" and may be affiliated with specific dealers, CarBargains is completely independent and does not take any money from dealers for steering buyers toward a particular dealer. CarBargains shops many different dealers to get its customers the best prices on new vehicles and is the only service that I recommend.

To see how CarBargains measured up to several other large car buying services, *Kiplinger's Personal Finance*

Magazine conducted a test for their December, 1992 publication. *Kiplinger's* used four services, including CarBargains, to shop for three popular cars: a Lexus LS 400 (retail $47,000), a Ford Taurus GL sedan (retail $18,393), and a Geo Prizm sedan (retail $11,907). At that time, many Lexus dealers were so confident they could sell their cars without cutting prices that they refused to deal with buying services. Only CarBargains was able to quote a lower price on the Lexus.

CarBargains
—Lexus: $5,704 below retail
—Taurus: $2,519 below retail
—Geo: $681 below retail

Amway Motoring Plan (members only)
—Lexus: no quote
—Taurus: $2,244 below retail
—Geo: $496 below retail

CarPuter (limited to approx. 500 dealers)
—Lexus: no quote
—Taurus: $2,298 below retail
—Geo: $598 below retail

Nationwide Auto Brokers
—Lexus: no quote
—Taurus: $2,212 below retail
—Geo: $561 below retail

As you can see, CarBargains was clearly the winner in the *Kiplinger's* test, resulting in dealer bids that were $83 to $185 lower than the other services on the Geo, $221 to $307 lower on the Taurus, and $5,704 lower on the Lexus.

In another test of car buying services done in 1992 by *The Washingtonian Magazine*, CarBargains got lower dealer bids than Price Club and the United Buying Service. The results of their test, shopping for a new Honda Civic sedan, are as follows:

CarBargains	$11,575
Price Club	$12,940
United Buying Service	$12,782

How CarBargains Works

CarBargains will make dealers compete with each other for your business, allowing you to avoid the unpleasant (and often costly) experience of negotiating on a new vehicle. They are so confident of their ability to get you the best possible deal that their service has a money-back guarantee: *If you are able to buy a car at a price lower then the best quote included in their report without using their information, they will gladly refund your entire fee.*

To use CarBargains, call toll-free (800) 475-7283. The fee for their service is $150 which can be paid by check or credit card. If you decide to order by mail, make your check payable to "CarBargains" and specify the year, make, and model of the vehicle you wish to buy. Include a daytime phone number and mail your request to:

CarBargains
733 15th Street NW, Suite 820
Washington, DC 20005

The following is a brief description of how the CarBargains service works:

1. You tell them the year, make, model, and style of the car or truck you wish to buy (for example, "1995 Ford Taurus 4-door sedan GL").

2. Within two weeks, CarBargains will get at least 5 dealers in your area to bid against each other on the vehicle you requested. Each dealer will commit to a specific dollar amount above (or below) the "factory invoice cost" on the vehicle.

3. You will receive a report that includes:

   • Dealer quote sheets showing how much above (or below) factory invoice cost each dealer has agreed to sell, and listing the names of the sales managers at each dealer responsible for the commitment.

   • Factory invoice cost information for your type of car or truck, showing what all dealers pay for the base vehicle and for each possible option.

   • Other useful information—on the value of your used car (based on a description you have given them), low-cost financing options, pros and cons of extended warranties/service contracts, how you may be able to get a service contract as good as your dealer offers at a substantially lower cost, etc.

4. You visit one or more of the dealers and...

   • Look at the vehicles on the lot;
   • Select the specific vehicle you want;
   • Use the information they've sent you to determine the factory invoice cost of the vehicle you've selected;
   • See the sales manager listed on your report's dealer

quote sheets and purchase the vehicle at the factory invoice cost plus (or minus) the amount agreed to by the dealer.

- If a vehicle with the options you want is not available on a dealer's lot, you can have the dealer order the vehicle (if available) from the factory, or from another dealer, at the agreed markup (or markdown) figure.

COMMON QUESTIONS
on CarBargains

Can't I do this myself?

Dealers know that CarBargains' bidding is for real—they know they will actually get at least 5 quotes. In addition, they know that a consumer who has paid for the CarBargains service is almost certain to buy immediately from one of the quoting dealers, so refusing to quote means losing a sale. However, when you call for a bid, the dealer may not believe that you will bother to get bids elsewhere. Worse yet, dealers often refuse to bid over the phone with consumers, using lines such as, "shop around, then come on down—we'll beat anyone else's price." They don't usually take "telephone shoppers" seriously.

Dealers know that CarBargains will get bids from other dealers, so each dealership knows it will have to bid real low to have any chance of winning. They remind dealers of any ongoing factory-to-dealer incentive programs, manufacturer holdbacks, carryover allowances, and other factors that give the dealer room to cut his price. Also, dealers know that if CarBargains doesn't get good prices locally, they will get quotes from dealers outside the area who will deliver locally.

CarBargains is a witness to the dealers' quotes; they get

signed commitments by fax and dealers know they will follow up. On the other hand, if a customer gets a quote by phone, some dealers may feel they can back out without serious consequences.

The CarBargains staff members are experts; they make sure all costs—advertising association fees, processing fees, dealer-installed options, etc.—are included in the dealers' bids, not added on later.

How close will the dealers be to my home?

CarBargains has a computer file of all dealers in the country. When you order their service, they identify dealers close to you and get them to bid. You can even have them include (or leave out) a dealer of your choice.

Do I have to decide which options I want before calling CarBargains?

No. You only need to tell them the year, make, model, and style of car you want. The dealers bid a specific dollar amount above (or below) the factory invoice cost. CarBargains will send you a factory invoice cost printout that shows you the invoice cost for the base vehicle and for each possible factory-installed option. This allows you to decide which options you want later, while still being able to figure out the total factory invoice cost.

Will I still get a factory rebate?

Your CarBargains report will tell you whether the car you are buying carries a factory-to-customer rebate. If it does, you will be able to get this rebate directly from the manufacturer, or you can have the dealer apply the rebate to your purchase price, further reducing the price of the car.

Is CarBargains able to get any car at a discount price?

Almost—the only car that's *never* available at a discount is a Saturn. Certain models that are in short supply may sell at a premium for a brief period (like the first Mazda Miatas), but most cars and trucks are available somewhere at a dealer who's willing to sell at a substantial discount.

How much can CarBargains save me on popular models?

Results will vary depending on the time of year, whether any factory-to-dealer incentives are in effect, and from one region to another. Each year there is relatively little discounting of new model-year vehicles in the first few months after introduction, but by November 1994 CarBargains was already finding many below-invoice deals on 1995 models. Examples cited by CarBargains include:

1995 Nissan 240SX	$1,600 below invoice
1995 Infiniti G20	$1,000 below invoice
1995 Mazda MPV	$500 below invoice
1995 Toyota Corolla	$400 below invoice
1995 Mercury Villager	$350 below invoice
1995 Cadillac Seville	$300 below invoice
1995 Chrysler LHS	$200 below invoice
1995 Mazda Protege	$200 below invoice
1995 Volvo 850	$100 below invoice
1995 Ford Windstar	$100 below invoice

However, some models are never sold below invoice. In some cases, the best available price may in fact be the full "window sticker" price, which may be 5% to 23% above the invoice cost, depending on the model. For example, in November 1994 the best prices the CarBargains competitive bidding process could find for some models were $1,000 or more above invoice—

1995 BMW 740i	$3,000 over invoice
1995 Infiniti Q45	$1,000 over invoice
1995 Lexus LS 400	$1,000 over invoice

As with any other product, car prices are simply determined by supply and demand, which change all the time. The key for the consumer is to find the best price available at any given time. The CarBargains service, which is the only service of its kind in the country, is designed to find that price by making car dealers "bid" for the consumer's business. It not only produces a good price, it also spares the consumer the hassles and high-pressure sales tactics often associated with buying a new car.

CHAPTER 13

Auto Brokers, Car Buying Services, & Membership Clubs

A number of "car buying" services have appeared on the national scene, taking advantage of consumers' distaste for negotiating with dealers. All of them promise substantial discounts on new cars and trucks—without the consumer doing any of the haggling—but results vary, sometimes dramatically. One service may be able to get a price that's hundreds less than the others and in some cases, a determined, knowledgeable consumer has negotiated a better price on his own than most of the services could get.

The following sections explain how the various services work—and why some work better than others. Potential problems associated with some services are also covered, and my personal recommendation is included.

Auto Brokers

Auto brokers and car buying services both claim to save consumers big money on the purchase of a new vehicle, but there are major differences in how they operate and make their money. These differences are significant and could affect not only the price you pay for a car, but what kind of service you receive after the purchase.

There are some companies using the name "broker" when they are actually operating as a buying service (for example, Nationwide Auto Brokers). Sometimes the only way to tell is to ask whether they are actually "buying and selling" or just "shopping for the best price." For the purpose of this discussion, an "auto broker" is a business that buys new cars from dealers to resell to consumers, and a "car buying service" is a business that shops around for the best price, then refers customers to specific dealers to buy the cars.

Auto brokers have been around for a long time, but they don't appear to have captured much of the car buying market. How they operate could be at least partially responsible for their lack of popularity. Brokers take orders from consumers, buy the cars from dealers (with the broker actually taking title to the vehicles), then resell the cars to consumers—after adding a "markup," of course.

When using a broker, the customer is usually required to put up either a large non-refundable deposit or the full purchase price before the car is ordered, creating a huge risk should something go wrong. Some (smaller) brokers have gotten into legal trouble for taking deposits, then failing to deliver the vehicles, causing some of their customers to lose large sums of money. For this reason, among others, I do not recommend the use of a true "broker."

Since brokers are not licensed to sell new cars, the broker actually becomes the "original owner" of the car, and the final customer is (legally) purchasing a "used" car. All original factory warranties do remain in effect for the final customer, though, and buyers can still get a "new car" loan rate.

Brokers usually buy from the same dealers, claiming to get low prices because of their "high volume." However, since they're not making a number of dealers compete with each other over every vehicle, it's doubtful that their prices are going to be the lowest available. Don't forget—it's competition that creates low prices, not "high volume."

Instead of receiving a fixed payment for negotiating a purchase, brokers make differing amounts of money based on the "spread" between their cost on the car and what the customer pays for it. A broker's desire to make a bigger profit is in direct conflict with the consumer's desire to get the lowest possible price, and since a broker is actually taking title and delivery of every vehicle he handles, he would have to make more money on a car than a buying service that is just shopping for the best price.

Another drawback to using auto brokers concerns their taking title to a car before reselling it to the consumer, making the broker the "original owner" of record with the manufacturer (just as a leasing company would be). In some cases, this may result in "less than great" service for a buyer who takes his car to a dealership that treats people better if they bought a car there, and worse yet, if they resent the fact that he used an auto broker.

When ordering a new vehicle through a broker, you will have less leverage to get things fixed before you take delivery. After all, the broker just ordered the car—he doesn't represent the manufacturer and he can't fix the car for you. You may be told, "Don't worry, let's just get all the paperwork done so you can take your new car home, then you'll have more time to look it over. Your local dealer will be glad to fix anything you find wrong, so there's no need to do that right now." (This may or may not be true.)

A potentially serious problem with being the "second owner" of a new car is that vehicle recall notices and other manufacturer communications are usually sent only to the original owner, so if they don't get forwarded, you may not find out that your car was recalled for a safety defect.

Car Buying Services

A number of car buying services have sprung up recently and are gaining in popularity. For a fee—anywhere from $49 to $150 or more—these services promise to save you big money on a new car by doing the negotiating for you. Many of them even offer a money-back guarantee that they can get you a better deal than you can get on your own.

Car buying services differ from true "brokers" in that a buying service does not actually buy or sell cars; instead, they get competing bids from dealers on the car you want. When they're through collecting bids (usually from four or five dealers), they turn them over to you to decide which dealer you want to use. You can then buy from the one with the lowest bid or use that bid to negotiate a better price with the dealer of your choice. The bids are usually from local dealerships, unless you specify how far you're willing to drive to save more money.

All that's left for you to do after you've selected a dealer is to decide whether you want to arrange your own financing or use the dealer's financing. Then you simply go to the dealer to sign the papers and pick up your new car.

There are many advantages to using a car buying service over an auto broker. Most people who use a buying service will end up getting their new car from a local dealership, so they should be treated just like anyone else who bought a car there if they need to go back later for service. Also, since no one else is first taking title to the car and reselling it, the consumer will be registered as the "original owner," ensuring that he will receive all recall notices and other factory correspondence pertaining to his car.

Since car buying services are only shopping around for the best prices, their overhead should be lower than that of auto brokers who actually buy the cars and take possession. Brokers obviously need to make more money on each car to cover the additional costs.

All car buying services are not alike. Some take money from dealers for steering customers their way (usually at least $200 per car), which not only increases the dealer's cost, but often the price to the customer as well. Buying services that charge the consumer less than $100 are usually being paid by dealers.

Some buying services protect their customers from "back-end sales" and some don't. If yours doesn't, you may be talked into buying several worthless and/or grossly overpriced services (like undercoating and extended warranties) when you go to pick up your car. Before you pay to use a service, ask how much information they provide regarding possible sales pitches in the finance and insurance office.

Another thing to watch out for at some car buying services is the offer of a "discount coupon book" for auto repairs and services. See the following section for details.

Club Discount Coupon Books

Discount coupons have been used by many well-known auto repair companies to lure consumers into their shops. In too many cases, unsuspecting motorists have been sold unnecessary repairs by mechanics and/or service advisors who were paid a sales commission or working under some type of sales quota. Contests have even been used to reward employees for selling more repairs than anyone else, a practice that encourages widespread fraud.

Two major car buying services—Consumers Car Club and AutoVantage—have set up membership clubs to save cardholders money on a variety of automotive services and repairs, through the use of a discount coupon book. While most of the businesses featured in their coupon books do have good reputations, they have included several national auto repair companies that have been accused of fraudulent business practices as a result of undercover investigations and/or class-action lawsuits.

> Note: The complete stories of the undercover investigations mentioned below—and many more— are contained in my first book, *What Auto Mechanics Don't Want You to Know.*

Consumers Car Club (also known as "the Car Club"). The coupon book provided by the Car Club includes discounts at Aamco Transmissions Centers. Aamco has repeatedly been accused of fraudulent business practices as a result of investigations by consumer protection agencies in 18 states. In California alone, 20 Aamco shops have been charged following undercover investigations.

AutoVantage. The coupon book provided by AutoVantage includes discounts at Aamco Transmissions Centers, Goodyear Auto Centers, and Kmart Auto Centers. As previously explained in the Car Club section, Aamco has repeatedly been accused of fraudulent business practices in the past.

Goodyear (company-owned) Auto Centers and Kmart Auto Centers are both targets of nationwide class-action lawsuits over allegations of fraudulent practices in their repair shops. The two companies are accused of creating an environment that resulted in the sale of unnecessary repairs through the use of sales commissions, quotas, and/or contests for the highest sales. Also, a number of Goodyear shops were recently accused of selling unnecessary repairs after undercover investigations were done in two states.

My Recommendation —

For those buyers who don't want to do battle with dealers, but would still like to save as much money as possible on a new car, I recommend using the CarBargains car buying service. They consistently get lower prices than the other services, they're not paid by dealers, and they also provide other valuable money-saving advice for consumers. (See Chapters 10 and 12 for more information.)

Warehouse Club Auto Buying Programs

The car buying programs set up by the discount warehouses typically have an agreement with only one dealership in each area for a particular type of vehicle, eliminating any competition between dealers for the same car. Members are guaranteed a price that is a specific dollar amount (usually $300 to $500) above the dealer invoice, even when there may be a dealer holdback and/or factory-to-dealer incentive that reduces the dealer's cost to $500 (or as much as $1,500) below invoice.

For example, the Price Club (now PriceCostco) Auto Buying Program for the San Francisco area was steering club members to a local Toyota dealer who had promised to sell Camrys for $399 *above* invoice. However, the CarBargains buying service obtained dealer bids for $600 *below* invoice for the same car, in the same area, at the same time. By making dealers compete for the business, CarBargains was able to get their customers prices that were $999 lower than Price Club on the same car.

Generally speaking, warehouse club auto buying programs are a lot better than paying suggested list (MSRP), but a good buying service — or a knowledgeable consumer — should be able to beat their prices.

Credit Union Buying Programs

Many credit unions (and other groups) have arranged for their members to have access to some type of discount car buying program. Some might use a local auto broker, others may use a buying service or program similar to the warehouse clubs. The prices obtained by some of these programs are not even as low as a knowledgeable consumer could get by negotiating on his own, so be sure to compare their prices with other services before making a commitment.

CHAPTER 14

Your New Car:
Taking Delivery

After all the negotiating is over and agreement has been reached on price and terms, there are still two things left to do before the dealer (and the salesman) can get paid—you have to sign the loan papers (or pay cash), and you have to sign the delivery receipt acknowledging that you have taken possession of your new car. Since this is your last opportunity to delay or cancel the sale, it's also the best time to pressure the dealer into fixing anything you find wrong with the car. Once you pay for and take delivery on your new car, you won't have as much leverage in getting defects fixed—especially flaws that are cosmetic instead of functional—so your predelivery inspection will be the last important thing you do in the car buying process.

The Predelivery Inspection

As the buyer of a new vehicle, you have the right to one that is free of all defects, from mechanical or functional problems to visual flaws related to "fit and finish." Before you pay for the car and sign the delivery receipt, be sure to perform a thorough inspection of the car, including a road test. If you discover any problems, insist that they be fixed before you take possession.

In order to get you to take delivery (so they can get paid), dealers will usually say, "Don't worry, everything will be fixed to your satisfaction later. All you have to do is bring the car back to our service department, and they'll fix anything that you find wrong. Plus, if you take the car home now, you'll have more time to look it over before you bring it back for servicing." Don't fall for this—insist that they correct all problems before you take possession.

Dealers are usually pretty good about repairing mechanical or functional problems on new cars, but when it comes to cosmetic items like upholstery, paint, and other "fit and finish" concerns, they can be very creative in trying to convince you that the flaw you noticed is normal. You may hear statements like "Oh, that's normal—they all look that way," or my personal favorite, "We can try to make it look better, but it could turn out worse than it is now, then you would have to live with it like that. If I were you, I would leave it alone—it's hardly noticeable." When in doubt, compare with similar new vehicles to see if the situation is normal, then refuse to take delivery if you're not satisfied.

Once you drive away in your new car, any scratches or dents will be assumed to be your fault, so be sure to do a thorough job on the visual inspection—both inside and out. Bring a friend or relative along to double-check for cosmetic flaws, and to help test the accessories and lights.

One last tip: Don't try to do a visual inspection at night—this needs to be done outside, in the sunlight, so make an appointment to do this at your convenience, when the weather is nice. Plan on spending a couple of hours, less if you have someone (not the salesman) to help you. When you're setting up a time to do the inspection, tell the salesman to leave the "dealer plates" on the car until after you're done with the predelivery inspection and road test. (When the salesman asks why, tell him you want to do the inspection and road test while the dealer still owns the car, in case you find something wrong. This might motivate him to make sure the car's in great shape before you get there.)

The following categories should be part of your predeliveryinspection:

Serial Number, Mileage, & Options. Be sure to check the serial number of the car you picked out against the one on the contract and the one they want you to drive home—they should all be the same. Note the odometer reading; if the car has more than 250-300 miles on it, demand a (believable) explanation. If they can't give you one, tell them to get you another car—that one was probably a "demo" that was loaned to employees for personal use. Confirm that all agreed-upon options are either on the car already or the contract specifies that they are to be installed later. (Don't rely on verbal promises; get everything in writing.)

Body & Paint. Inspect all exterior paint, chrome, and trim items for flaws. Look for uneven surfaces, mismatched paint, and other evidence of repainting or touchup, as this could indicate a previously-damaged vehicle that should have been disclosed. (Dealers are required by law to give buyers written disclosure on cars that have had body damage repaired.) Your new car should not have any scratches, dents, or paint flaws—unless you're getting a reduced price to compensate for them.

Minor paint scratches can usually be buffed out, but the car may need repainting if it has deep scratches or other paint flaws. If this is the case, refuse the car and insist that they give you another one—it's almost impossible to repaint part (or all) of a new car and have it look as good as a factory paint job. Even if it does look good immediately after it's repainted, chances are that several years later, after the paint has"aged" in the sun, it won't match perfectly anymore.

Fit and Finish. Inspect the "fit and finish" on all exterior and interior items. The doors, trunk, and hood should open and close smoothly and all sheet metal edges should be flush after they are closed. Check the spacing at the sides of the doors and around the trunk and hood—it should be even all the way around. Make sure all movable windows (and sun/moonroof, if equipped) operate smoothly. Check all of the seat belts and seat mechanisms (tracks, motors, recliners, adjustable headrests, etc.) for proper operation. Inspect all upholstery and carpet for defects, poor fit, stains, excess glue, etc. Don't forget to check the headliner (that's the fabric used to cover up the interior side of the roof).

Equipment and Accessories. Have the salesman show you how to operate all of the accessories: lights; stereo; power locks, seats, and windows; air conditioning; cruise control; windshield washers and wipers; rear window defroster; sunroof/moonroof; remote mirrors; security system; etc. Then try them yourself to verify that everything works properly.

This next step involves the help of the friend or relative who came with you. Check all of the lights on the car—headlights, taillights, brake lights, turn signals, emergency flasher, interior and courtesy lights, trunk light, engine compartment light, etc.

Under the Hood. Once again, have the salesman show you how to check all of the fluid levels, where the dipsticks are located, and where to add fluids. Low fluid levels could indicate a leak—or just sloppy new car preparation. Either way, call it to the dealer's attention. If you find several things wrong, tell them to send it back to new car prep for a more thorough job. When you're sure all the fluid levels are OK, do a quick visual check of the tires (all four tires should be the same brand and size, properly inflated), then you're ready for the final phase of the inspection—the road test.

The Road Test. A thorough road test should be done to detect any performance problems related to the engine, transmission, steering, and brakes. Accelerate briskly from a stop, running through all the gears, then drive at a steady speed. Does the car run smoothly with plenty of power? If it has an automatic transmission, does it shift smoothly?

Take the car through several turns or curves to check the steering and suspension. Does the car handle well? Does it recover quickly after turning? Drive the car at about 30-35 mph on a straight, flat road, then let go of the steering wheel (momentarily). The car should continue traveling in a straight line. If it pulls to one side, the front end alignment should be checked.

Check the brakes under both light and heavy application. The car should stop smoothly and there should be no brake noises or pulsating (unless the car has ABS). On vehicles with Anti-lock Brake Systems, the brake pedal will pulsate during hard braking as the solenoids cycle the hydraulic pressure on and off to prevent wheel lock-up.

To check for squeaks and rattles, drive the car on a bumpy road. Be sure to check the operation of the cruise control and other accessories while driving, and take notes on any problems or noises that were discovered on the road test.

When you're done with the inspection and road test, have the dealer make a copy of your "defect list," then tell him to call you after they've fixed everything on the list. Do another quick inspection to make sure the repairs were done, then check the body and paint to make sure the car didn't get any new dents or scratches while it was in the service department. If everything is OK, you're ready to make your down payment, sign the loan papers and the delivery receipt, then drive home in your new car.

CHAPTER 15

Service Department Secrets

Back in the "good old days" (for car dealers), new-car sales were so profitable that many dealers looked at their service departments as existing just to service new cars and perform warranty work. Customers who bought cars from a dealer were usually treated better in the service department than those who didn't, since the dealer was really only interested in selling more cars. If he occasionally made some money from paying service customers, that was just icing on the cake, but there was little interest in expanding the service department.

Manufacturers estimate that only 30% of car buyers return to dealers for service after their warranty runs out. Some people still complain of poor service and high prices, and the experiences of many across the country who have run into callous service people in the past is going to take a long time to overcome.

Well, there may be good news for consumers who would like to go back to the dealer for service, if only they could be sure they would receive better treatment. The good news—for paying customers—is that dealers now care about winning your service business *because they need the money*. New-car profits are down because people are keeping their cars longer and there are too many dealers selling the same cars, so competition is keeping prices down. Service and parts made up about 50% of the average dealer's profit in 1993, so they can't afford to turn their backs on paying service customers anymore.

Although some dealers still have a long way to go before their service departments can claim to have a good reputation, it looks like many have been moving in the right direction. In the September 1994 issue of *Consumer Reports,* the results of their Annual Questionnaire were published, analyzing readers' experiences with repair shops between 1991 and 1993. To arrive at an overall satisfaction rating, shops were graded on median prices, repeat problems with the repair, pressure to sell additional parts, and whether the job was completed on time.

The results of the Consumer Reports survey were: Out of 22,000 responses from readers whose cars had brake repairs, independent repair shops came in first in overall customer satisfaction, with a median brake price of $150. Dealership service departments came in second, with a median brake price of $200.

Major chain stores scored much lower in overall customer satisfaction, due to more sales pressure, repeat problems, and jobs not completed when promised. Midas Muffler & Brake Shops came in 5th ($180), Goodyear Auto Service—6th ($170), Firestone Mastercare Service Centers—7th ($180), and Sears Auto Centers came in 8th (last place) with a median price of $200.

As you can see, dealerships actually rate higher in overall customer satisfaction than the major chain stores (in general). Of course, there are always exceptions, but if a particular dealer has a bad reputation for service, that will usually be common knowledge in the local community. Also, the local Better Business Bureau can provide a rating (by phone) as to how the dealer resolves complaints filed against his business.

Now that I've detailed the progress many dealers have made in cleaning up their image, it's time to cover the pros and cons of using dealer service departments, as well as the common tricks some of them have used (in the past) to take advantage of people. Since there are still some dealers out there who would rather have your money than a good reputation, you need to know how they operate so you'll be able to identify them before it's too late.

Pros & Cons of Service Departments

Many vehicle owners will not use new car dealership service departments for two reasons--one, because they think that dealerships charge too much, and two, because they're not able to talk directly to the mechanic who will be working on their car.

The perception that dealerships charge too much is often a result of past experiences people have had combined with a comparison of prices charged by independents and dealerships. As a general rule, the posted hourly labor rates at most independent repair shops are lower than those at most dealership service departments.

There are several reasons why dealerships often charge more than other shops. The first one is higher overhead; mechanics in dealerships are often paid more (and have more benefits) than mechanics working in other repair shops, and dealerships usually have a lot more expensive equipment that is required to work on newer models.

Another reason for dealership prices being higher is that their service departments are not usually willing to give away any parts or labor on a job that turns out to be more difficult or expensive than originally estimated. Because each department's profitability in a dealership is constantly monitored by upper management (and accountants), service personnel will usually do whatever it takes to make a profit on every job.

On the other hand, many independent shops will absorb the additional time that is required to finish a difficult job, and will sometimes even give away parts to avoid creating an unpleasant customer relations problem. (When things go wrong, as they often do in the auto repair business, most shops would rather lose money on a job than lose a good customer.)

Many independent shops don't even know how much they need to charge just to stay in business. Some of them have a vague idea, but they're afraid to charge that much for fear of losing customers. Because of this, a great number of independent shops are so unprofitable that they are inches away from going out of business. Many shops do go out of business; some survive by working long hours, employing lower-paid (i.e., less-skilled) mechanics, and not upgrading shop equipment.

The advantages of using a dealership service department (that sells your type of vehicle) include: expert knowledge of your vehicle (at least in theory), factory technical information and assistance, factory-trained mechanics (again, in theory), the use of original-equipment parts, and the availability of binding arbitration.

Binding arbitration (through Autocap) is usually available to resolve disputes between dealerships and consumers. There is usually no charge to consumers for this service, and it can save the time and expense of going to court. Decisions are binding on the dealership, but not on the consumer, who is free to take his case to court if he is not satisfied.

Dealership mechanics are *usually* specialists in one repair area of one brand of vehicles (for example, one mechanic might repair transmissions only, while another mechanic might only repair computer systems). Because they have access to factory training and technical assistance that is not usually available to mechanics working in independent shops, they are *usually* more knowledgeable concerning the types of vehicles they work on.

As stated earlier, one of the reasons that dealerships have higher overhead is that their mechanics are usually paid more than those working in other repair shops. Generally speaking, dealership mechanics are paid more because they have had more training and are more skilled in their particular area. (They have to be pretty sharp to repair new cars.)

While it is true that consumers are more likely to find highly-skilled technicians (for a particular vehicle) at a dealership, it's not true that *all* mechanics working in dealerships are highly skilled. There is a serious shortage of top-notch mechanics and dealerships are affected, too. I have met quite a few dealership mechanics who are highly-skilled, but I have also seen many who were fairly incompetent.

In the past, I've had to repair many vehicles that were misdiagnosed or "hacked over" by dealership mechanics. Some good examples of this involved mechanics who replaced 6 or 8 computer parts on a vehicle before the problem was fixed. (Although it's sometimes necessary to replace 2 or 3 parts to repair a computer system, the only situation that would justify replacing that many parts would be if the engine caught on fire and all those parts were burned.)

Even though a dealership's posted labor rate may be higher than the labor rate at other repair shops, a dealership can still perform some types of repairs for less money. This is especially true of repairs on computer systems and other "high-tech" items on late-model vehicles. A factory-trained specialist should be able to diagnose and repair difficult problems much faster than a mechanic who works on several (or many) different types of vehicles.

Sometimes a mechanic has to make an educated guess concerning which part to replace. This is where a dealership mechanic has a distinct advantage over an independent—he can usually borrow a new part from the parts department to see if that will cure the problem, and if it doesn't, he can usually return it so the customer won't have to pay for it.

Independent shops can't borrow parts. Once a part is installed, they have to keep it, which means that the customer will have to pay for it even if it didn't cure the problem. This can sometimes result in consumers paying more for repairs at an independent shop than they would have paid at a dealership.

If a particular problem is common to one model, the manufacturer may repair it for free, even though the official written warranty has expired. (This is known as a "secret warranty.") For example, I have seen Toyota dealerships replace some exhaust manifolds on vehicles with 100,000 miles on them, at no charge to the customer. These types of repairs are not widely known outside of dealerships, so customers may end up paying for repairs at independent shops that could have been done for free.

Even though dealerships have factory training and other advantages, they still have trouble finding and keeping good mechanics just like any other business. Sometimes new mechanics just don't work out, and a bad one can mess up a lot of cars before he is fired. One local dealership couldn't perform any smog inspections for a while because it didn't have any mechanics who could pass the new state test for a smog license.

The disadvantages of using a dealership service department (that sells your type of vehicle) include: repair bills that are often higher than independent shops for the same repair, not being able to talk to the person who is going to work on your vehicle, and sometimes encountering an indifferent attitude concerning the cost of repairs and whether they will be completed on time.

Posted Labor Rates vs. Actual Labor Rates

One of the things to watch out for at dealership service departments is when their posted labor rate is lower than their actual labor rate (based on actual time spent on the job). For example, an independent repair shop that has a posted labor rate of $50 per hour may charge $75 labor for a front brake job, because the job takes 1.5 hours. However, a dealership with a posted labor rate of $50 per hour may charge $100 labor for the same job, making their actual labor rate $66 per hour, because it's still only a 1.5 hour job.

This is a fairly common practice, resulting in so many complaints that dealerships in some states are now required to post a notice explaining that their labor charges are based on "established times" for particular repairs and may be higher than the posted labor rates for the actual time spent working on a vehicle.

When this method of pricing is used, consumers are not able to make accurate price comparisons based on the posted labor rates. If you call a dealership (or any other shop) to compare prices, make sure you get the total labor charges for a particular repair, as well as a breakdown of the parts to be changed (and their prices) so you can tell what the actual labor rates are.

Charging for Warranty Work

Another thing to watch out for at dealership service departments is the practice of charging for diagnosis and/or repairs that should be covered under the warranty. One way this is done is when consumers bring their vehicles in for repairs without knowing that they are covered under the warranty, and the service personnel fail to mention it, so the vehicle owners end up paying for the repairs.

The other way this is done is when consumers expect the repairs to be done under the warranty, but they are given a phony story explaining why the repairs aren't covered or why they'll have to pay for diagnosis. (If a dealership tries to pull this scam on you, ask to speak to the service manager, and if he doesn't resolve the problem to your satisfaction, call the manufacturer's customer service number for assistance.) The following true story of a dealership that tried to pull this scam on me illustrates how this is done.

> When my car was about three years old, I took it to a local dealership to have some repairs done that were covered by the 5 year/50,000 mile emissions warranty. The service writer told me that I would have to pay $50 (for 1 hour of labor) to diagnose the problem, then if it turned out that the problem was covered by the warranty, the actual repairs would be free, but I would still have to pay the $50 charge for diagnosis.
>
> At this point, I told the service writer that I had worked in several dealerships as a mechanic, and none of them had charged for diagnosis of problems that were covered under warranty. As soon as he heard that, he said, "Well, if it turns out that the problem is covered by the warranty, you won't be charged for the diagnostic time." When I picked up my car at the end of the day, the diagnostic charge had been crossed off and the repairs were done under the warranty.

That service writer insisted on charging me for diagnosing the problem, even though it was covered by the warranty.

(Fortunately, I knew better.) I don't believe it was just an honest mistake, because he had worked there for about 8 years and seemed to be fairly knowledgeable concerning late-model cars.

Why would a dealership try to charge customers for repairs that could be done under warranty? Two possible reasons: 1) Because the dealer can file a warranty claim anyway and get paid twice for the same repair, and 2) dealers make more money per hour on cash customers than they do on warranty work.

The car manufacturers set limits on how much time they will pay for each repair done under warranty, effectively lowering the amount received by the dealer for every hour worked. For example, a manufacturer may only pay for one-half hour of diagnostic time (even if it takes an hour) for a particular problem under warranty, but a dealership could charge a cash customer one hour or more to diagnose the same problem.

As you can see, dealerships have a major financial incentive to charge customers for repairs that could be done under warranty, so it's wise to question or challenge them if they try to charge you for something that you think should be done for free. If all else fails, call the manufacturer's customer service number for assistance before paying for diagnosis or repairs.

Charging for Unnecessary Maintenance

Another outrageous practice at some service departments involves charging for scheduled maintenance that the manufacturers say does not need to be done for another 15,000 to 30,000 miles or more. This often involves replacement of parts that could easily last 10,000 to 15,000 miles or more, and in many cases the parts could be replaced for free (under warranty), if they really were defective.

To illustrate how this scam works, we'll use a "typical" 15,000 mile service. On many cars, the service recommended by the manufacturer might only be a routine oil and oil filter change, and maybe a tire rotation. A dealer who wants to "increase his cashflow" would also replace the spark plugs, distributor cap and rotor, ignition wires, filters, coolant, and/or transmission fluid. He might even align the front end. So, instead of paying $30 to $40 for the factory-recommended service, the customer may pay as much as $300 to $400—for unnecessary repairs.

According to an article titled, "Made-up Maintenance" that appeared in the September 14, 1992 issue of *U.S. News & World Report*, the above practice seems to be fairly common. The magazine's investigation included a survey that was done to find out what services dealers perform during "scheduled maintenance" visits. *U.S. News* surveyed 122 dealers in seven major cities across the country, gathering estimates for service on six popular late-model cars. Almost 80% of the dealers they surveyed added services to the manufacturers list; 60% also included replacement of parts that the manufacturer said did not need replacing.

In the article, several dealers tried to defend the additional services, offering excuses of "hot summers, cold winters, humidity, stop-and-go driving," etc. Officials from two auto makers disagreed. Mazda's manager of quality assurance was quoted as saying, "Every town has traffic, and most areas have periods of stop-and-go...we don't build cars that are going to have problems because of commuting or air temperature or salt on the roads a few times a year."

The *U.S. News* article also claimed that Ford's parts and service engineering manager said dealers may, on occasion, have reason to exceed the manufacturer's maintenance schedule. He gave an example of plugged fuel filters caused by poor local fuel quality that could result in driveability problems, a case that would justify more frequent replacement of fuel filters. [In his example, affected vehicles would exhibit symptoms indicating that a problem exists *before* a vehicle is brought in for routine service.] The Ford manager also said that manufacturer's "severe-service" schedules were designed to include traffic, dust, extreme weather and other harsh conditions, so it's usually a waste of money to let a dealer talk you into additional services.

Two other practices to watch out for were also mentioned in the *U.S. News* article: inflated labor times and "ghost services." The first involves charging several more hours of labor for easy-to-perform services like rotating the tires; changing the brake fluid; adding [usually worthless] additives to the oil, fuel, and cooling systems; and performing quick visual inspections of the suspension and drivetrain.

"Ghost services" refer to the outrageous practice of charging for work done on items that can't be serviced, don't need to be serviced, or worse yet—don't even exist. In the *U.S. News* survey, 29% of the Mazda dealers included a valve adjustment in their 15,000 mile service, and 38% included it at 30,000 miles. However, according to the manufacturer, all Mazda cars produced in the last five years have self-adjusting valves, including the model used in the survey. [That means the valves can't be adjusted.] Some other popular ghost services: cleaning/adjusting the choke on fuel-injected cars (that have no choke), and adjusting the idle speed on computer-controlled cars (where the idle speed is controlled by the computer).

Aside from the "minor" issues of fairness, honesty, and general ethics in business, the practice of "made-up maintenance" can actually be against the law if customers are told that parts are bad, and they're not. Shops that recommend unnecessary repairs can find themselves in serious trouble. The following stories of two dealerships that were accused of doing just that illustrate some of the practices consumers should guard against.

Undercover Investigation, 1989-90
Lodi Honda, California

After receiving a consumer complaint against a Honda car dealership in Lodi, California, the Bureau of Automotive Repair and the San Joaquin County district attorney's office conducted an undercover investigation. When the investigation was completed, the district attorney's office filed a consumer protection lawsuit against Lodi Honda, an independently-owned new car dealership, asking for civil penalties of $1 million.

Lodi Honda was accused of charging over 2,000 customers for service that was either unnecessary or never done. According to the Bureau, undercover agents took several Hondas to the dealership, requesting that 30,000 mile services be performed. The Bureau's report claimed that Lodi Honda personnel performed service that was not recommended by Honda Motor Corp. until 45,000 and 60,000 miles. The report also claimed that those services were not explained to investigators until after they had been done. Bureau officials said that they inspected a vehicle after the service appointment and found that some services listed as being completed were not done.

The Bureau's report concluded: "This constitutes fraud, false and misleading statements, and false and misleading documents. It is apparent that Lodi Honda is engaging in unethical and unfair business practices, in that they are charging for services and receiving higher profits at the expense of the consumer."

The owner of Lodi Honda agreed to pay a total of

$170,000 to settle the charges. ($20,000 for civil penalties, $35,000 for investigative and legal costs, $115,000 for restitution)

Undercover Investigation, 1989-90
Gene Gabbard Honda, California

In a similar case, the owner of Gene Gabbard Honda in Stockton was sued by the District Attorney's office in 1990 over the alleged sale of unnecessary parts while performing 15,000; 30,000; and 45,000 mile services. The Bureau of Automotive Repair said the undercover vehicles they sent in for service already had new spark plugs, distributor rotors, and fuel filters, but they were replaced anyway. The alleged overcharges varied from $40-60 for approximately 400 customers. To settle the charges, the dealership agreed to pay a total of $61,000 which included more than $21,000 in restitution.

How to Protect Yourself

To guard against these practices, consumers should check their owners' manuals to verify that the recommended services are actually required to keep up the warranty.

Most tune-up parts, including spark plugs, distributor rotor and cap, and ignition wires are covered under the emission warranty for the first 30,000 miles (or whenever the manufacturer recommends the first scheduled replacement).

Emission control and computer system parts are covered under warranty for 5 years or 50,000 miles on pre-1990 cars and light/medium duty trucks. For 1990 and newer models, all emission control and computer system parts are covered under warranty for 3 years or 50,000 miles; the repair or replacement of some high-priced defective parts listed in the owner's manual may be covered up to 7 years or 70,000 miles.

Note on Scheduled Maintenance

Vehicle owners do not have to take their cars to a dealer for scheduled maintenance. (It's against the law for them to require that, unless they're going to do the repairs for free.) All that's needed to keep your warranty in effect is to have all the scheduled maintenance done, on time, by a licensed repair facility. Be sure to keep good records, in case the manufacturer or dealer tries to get out of a warranty repair by claiming that your car wasn't properly maintained. And yes, you can change your own oil without voiding your warranty. Just keep the receipts for the oil and filters, and make sure it's done properly.

CHAPTER 16

Complaints, Lemon Laws, & Other Recourse

What can you do if things go wrong with your car, but the dealer can't (or won't) repair it to your satisfaction? Or worse yet, what if your new car is spending more time in the shop than in your driveway, and you're beginning to suspect that it may be a lemon? If it turns out to be a lemon, are you stuck with it?

A number of government agencies exist to help consumers who have disputes with automotive businesses. In addition, numerous independent consumer-advocate groups have sprung up to pressure government agencies to take action on particular issues. These outside groups can also provide valuable information and assistance for consumers who haven't yet found solutions to their automotive problems.

Consumers often have specific rights and protections under the law, but those rights and protections will vary from state to state. For example, there are no federal laws covering "lemons," but all 50 states have their own lemon laws on the books. Most states also have general "business and professions" laws against deceptive or fraudulent business practices, but only two states (California and

Michigan) have separate auto repair agencies to monitor and investigate the shops within their borders.

To find out what specific laws govern the automotive businesses in your state, contact your state attorney general's consumer protection division.

Initial Complaints

The following advice is intended for situations where consumers have no reason to believe that fraud is involved. If you do suspect fraud or other dishonest business practices, contact your local district attorney's office or your state attorney general.

I'm a firm believer that anyone can make an honest mistake, so my advice for consumers regarding their first problem with a business is to immediately voice their complaint with someone in management who has enough authority to handle the problem. In a small business, this may be the owner, but in a large business like a car dealer, you may not be able to speak to the owner. (It's worth a try, though.) The service manager is the head of his department, the sales manager is the top guy for sales, and the general manager is the head of the whole dealership (he reports directly to the owner). Those department heads have authority to resolve difficult problems.

Let's use a repair situation as an example of how to get a problem resolved. You took your car to the dealer's service department to get something repaired, they charged you for it, but it's still not fixed. What do you do? Remember my initial advice—don't start screaming (yet), be polite (at least the first time). Give them the benefit of the doubt and a chance to resolve the problem in a way that's fair to you. If the service advisor can arrange this (in a reasonable length of time), let him, but if he starts making excuses, tell him you want to speak to the service manager. Don't accept the service advisor's word as final, especially when you don't think you're being treated fairly.

If the service manager fails to resolve the problem to your satisfaction, then ask for the general manager (or the owner). If no one in the dealership will resolve your problem, ask for the name and phone number of the manufacturer's zone manager. The zone manager can often find solutions to difficult problems, but don't forget that part of his job is to save the company money. (A cynic would describe the zone manager's job as existing to keep customers as happy as possible, while spending as little of the company's money as possible.) After the zone manager, any further complaints should be sent to the company president.

Be polite, but confident and aggressive. In dealing with all levels of management, let them know that you demand satisfaction and you're not going to give up until you get it. (Remember—"the squeaky wheel gets the grease.") At each step, when you run into roadblocks, always ask for the name and phone number of that person's boss. Let them know you're going to complain to upper management.

Playing Hardball

Threatening to file complaints with government agencies can sometimes be effective, especially if you have a good case against the dealer. (The agencies are listed in this chapter.) However, you may be told, "Go ahead, we don't care." In that case, tell them you're going to write letters to the owner of the dealership *and* the president of the car company, letting them know how unhappy you are with the car and the treatment you received.

Get the names of the managers you dealt with to let

them know they will be included in your complaint letters, then ask them for the name and address of the company president so they know you're really going to write. Tell them you're never going to buy another car from their company because of the way you were treated. (Mention one of their competitors who will be getting your future business—they hate hearing that.) Also mention that you're going to be telling everyone you know how badly you were treated, warning them not to buy cars there.

One last tip for extreme cases: Ask the dealer how he would like having you—and your friends—picketing in front of his business every Saturday and Sunday, carrying signs displaying your grievance. (Saturdays and Sundays are the biggest sale days of the week, so that's the best time to picket.) If you have one of those local "action line" TV programs, they might want to get involved, so let the dealer know that you intend to contact them.

Picketing can be very effective in getting problems resolved, but you usually have to follow through on your threat. If you decide to picket, just make sure you stay off the dealer's property—he can have you arrested for trespassing. The sidewalk, however, is usually public property, so that's where to picket. (To be safe, ask the city or county first.) Recruit some friends to help out, bring a picnic lunch, and have fun—remember, the first amendment guarantees that you have the right to free speech, as long as it's true.

If you've struck out at this point, your last resort is to go to court. For minor issues, small claims court can be relatively quick and inexpensive, since no lawyers are allowed in court. For bigger problems, you may need a lawyer. Your local bar association should have a referral service that can set up a low-cost initial consultation with an attorney who specializes in automotive issues. Consumers with good cases can often get attorneys to represent them on a contingency basis. The Center for Auto Safety also offers attorney referrals for lemon law cases.

Mediation/Arbitration

A number of mediation and arbitration programs are also available to help solve consumers' car problems without going to court, but some of them can take months (and months) to reach a conclusion. The national programs usually only handle problems related to factory warranty repairs and defective vehicles (lemons), while some of the local programs may also handle car sales and general repair complaints. Local and state-run arbitration programs seem to be more "consumer-friendly" than national ones, so call your state attorney general's office (and your local Better Business Bureau) to find out if they've set up a program.

If you decide to use arbitration, make sure any decision that is made will only be binding on the manufacturer or dealer, and not on you. A good program will allow the consumer to take his case to court if he doesn't like the final arbitration decision. Check out the program before you make a commitment, and make sure you understand how it works.

Then do your homework: Organize your receipts and repair orders, make an outline of the car's history, and try to locate documents that will back up your case. Write to the Center for Auto Safety for any information they may have on your car, then ask your local dealer and zone manager for any technical service bulletins that mention your particular problem. (You can also get these from the National Highway Traffic Safety Administration.) Include copies of your records and other documents with your application (keep the originals). Request copies of everything submitted by the other side and challenge items you think are incorrect. Don't be afraid to send in additional supporting documents after you've filed your application, just ask that they be included in your file. And be sure to include a copy of your warranty (and your state's lemon law provisions, if applicable).

In the event the arbitrator rules against you, ask how to file an appeal. (You may not be allowed to do this if you've already accepted the decision, so be sure to check out your options before agreeing to anything.) Just because you lost in arbitration doesn't mean you didn't have a good case. After initially losing in arbitration, some consumers have won large judgements against automakers by taking their cases to court.

Lemon Laws

"Lemon laws" are state laws giving consumers specific rights when they have purchased a new car that requires too many repairs within a certain time period. All 50 states have their own lemon laws, but there aren't any federal laws in this area, so specific rules and remedies will vary from state to state. Less than half of the states include leased vehicles in their lemon laws, so be sure to check the laws in your state to see whether your "lemon" is covered.

The following description is a typical lemon law, but some details may be different in your state: A new car that is sold with a manufacturer's written warranty may be returned to the manufacturer for a refund (or replacement) if it can't be repaired. 1) The problems must be covered by the warranty and they must substantially reduce the vehicle's safety, value, or use to the consumer. 2) The manufacturer (or its agents) must have made four or more attempts to repair the same problem, or the vehicle must have been out of service for a total of 30 days (not necessarily in a row) while being repaired for any number of problems. 3) The "30 days out of service" or the four repair attempts must have occurred within the first 12 mos. or 12,000 miles, whichever occurs first. 4) The consumer has directly notified the manufacturer about the problems, if required to do so by the warranty materials or the owner's manual.

If all four of the above conditions exist for a vehicle, a lemon law may presume that the vehicle owner is entitled to a refund or replacement. For manufacturers that provide a certified arbitration program, consumers must first submit their disputes to the program before they are allowed to use the lemon law presumption in a lawsuit against the manufacturer.

To find out how the lemon law works in your state, contact your state attorney general's office or the state department of consumer affairs. You can also write to the Center for Auto Safety.

Auto Repair Tips

Be sure to keep an accurate record of your repair experiences. Take notes. Insist on a written repair order for all repairs, even those done for free under warranty. (You may need those records later to prove that the problem was never really fixed, or that you had too many problems with the same car.) All repair orders should contain the date, mileage, and symptom/problem.

Save all receipts and repair orders, and don't allow a shop to keep your only copy of a repair order—make a copy first, then keep the original for yourself. That way you won't find yourself in the helpless position of having no written record of the repairs done to your car.

To avoid being charged for repairs that aren't needed, make sure the inital repair order accurately describes the problem or symptoms you want repaired. If your car's engine dies at stops, don't tell them you want a tune-up, tell them to write up the repair as "diagnose: dies at stops." That way, if they tell you a particular part is causing the problem, and it turns out they're wrong, you'll have written proof that they made a mistake. If it becomes necessary, you can use this in small-claims court to get your money back.

Who to Call

AUTO REPAIR COMPLAINTS

CALIFORNIA—
Bureau of Automotive Repair
10240 Systems Parkway
Sacramento, CA 95827
Calif. only (800) 952-5210
All others (916) 445-1254

MICHIGAN—
Bureau of Automotive Regulation
208 N. Capitol Ave.
Lansing, MI 48918
Mich. only (800) 292-4204
All others (313) 357-5108

ALL OTHER STATES—
Contact your state Consumer Protection Agency,
or the state Attorney General's office

For complaints against auto repair shops, call or write the appropriate agency for your state. Complaint forms can usually be requested by phone. Action can be taken for obvious violations of a state's laws or regulations. If numerous complaints are filed against one shop, an investigation may be started.

Complaints can also be made to your local Better Business Bureau and city/county District Attorney's consumer protection division.

NEW & USED CARS

SALES PRACTICES—

Complaints regarding questionable sales practices at new or used car dealers should be sent to:

—Local/State Department of Motor Vehicles,
    Bureau of Investigations
—State New Motor Vehicle Board
—Local District Attorney's office
—State Attorney General's office

WARRANTY PROBLEMS, ORIGINAL & EXTENDED—

Complaints regarding a manufacturer's or dealer's failure to honor the original warranty, extended warranty, or service contract should be sent to:

—Manufacturer and/or dealer (by certified mail)
—Local/State Department of Motor Vehicles,
    Bureau of Investigations
—State New Motor Vehicle Board
—Local Consumer Affairs agency

MEDIATION & ARBITRATION—

Better Business Bureau
Auto Line (800) 955-5100

The Better Business Bureau Auto Line provides information on mediation and arbitration services for a number of automakers. Complaints are limited to manufacturers' defects for cars under warranty, although many companies allow a grace period of up to 6 months.

Your local BBB may also offer mediation and arbitration for disputes with participating dealers and repair shops. They can also record complaints against local businesses and report how complaints have been handled. Contact your local office for details.

STATE-RUN ARBITRATION PROGRAMS—

Over a dozen states have set up their own arbitration programs, and these are usually more "consumer-friendly" than the national ones. To find out if your state has one, contact your state Attorney General's office.

MEDIATION & ARBITRATION—

AUTOCAP
National Automobile Dealers Association
8400 Westpark Drive
McLean, VA 22102
(703) 821-7144

AUTOCAP provides third party mediation for sales and

service problems with manufacturers or dealers. Arbitration is also available for unresolved problems.

Note: Since AUTOCAP is a voluntary program run by state and local dealer associations, some dealers may not participate. In addition, many AUTOCAP programs do not follow the arbitration guidelines required for warranty cases by the FTC.

LEMON LAWS, SECRET WARRANTIES, VEHICLE DEFECTS, SAFETY RECALLS—

Center for Auto Safety
2001 S Street NW, Suite 410
Washington, DC 20009
(202) 328-7700

The Center for Auto Safety is a non-profit clearing house for information on lemon laws, secret warranties, vehicle defects, recalls, and attorney referral to lemon law specialists. To receive information, send a self-addressed, stamped envelope to the Center with a note listing the year, make, and model of your vehicle. Don't forget to specify what kind of information you need. (Normal response time is 3-4 weeks.)

FACTORY RECALLS, SAFETY DEFECTS, & SERVICE BULLETINS—

National Highway Traffic Safety Administration
400 7th Street SW, Room 5110
Washington, DC 20590
Auto Safety Hotline (800) 424-9393

The NHTSA collects information on all automotive recalls (including child safety seats), safety defects and complaints, crash tests, standards for all automotive parts, and factory service bulletins covering all vehicles sold in the United States. Will research service bulletins to locate those explaining a manufacturer's solution to a difficult repair problem. Has certified data and films on crash tests. **Be sure to notify NHTSA if you discover a manufacturer's defect that could impair the safety of your vehicle.**

On GM, FORD, and VW vehicles, factory service bulletin information can also be obtained by calling the following manufacturers' toll-free customer service numbers:
GM (800) 551-4123; FORD (800) 241-3673;
VW (800) 544-8021.

If you need to get recall or service bulletin information immediately, any repair shop with an Alldata computerized information system can print them out for you (typical charge: $10-15). To locate a shop near you, call Alldata Corp. at (800) 829-8727, select "operator."

**VEHICLE DEFECTS,
CONSUMER COMPLAINTS,
& ARBITRATION INFO—**

Federal Trade Commission
6th & Pennsylvania Avenue, NW
Washington, DC 20580
(202) 326-2000

The FTC investigates unfair or deceptive trade practices in the sale and repair of automobiles. Complaints regarding these practices should be filed with the Commission. The FTC also collects information and complaints regarding vehicle defects, which can be used to force automakers to offer free repairs for common problems. Information on arbitration is also available.

EMISSION WARRANTIES —

Environmental Protection Agency
401 M Street SW
Washington, DC 20460
(202) 233-9040

The EPA has complete information on all vehicle emission warranties, gas mileage data for all vehicles, and import/export emission information.

What Car Dealers Don't Want You to Know

CHAPTER 17

Tips for Used Car Buyers

Buying a good late-model, low-mileage, used car instead
of a new one can go a long way toward keeping your driving costs down. For owners of new cars, the biggest expense is depreciation, with a car suffering its biggest drop
in value during the first 2 to 3 years. So, let the first owner pay for that, then step in and buy the car at a big discount from its original price.

Previous lease vehicles can offer great value for a low
price. The market value of a 2-year old lease vehicle will
be about 35-50% below original retail even though it's still
in excellent condition with low mileage. It will cost a lot
less over time to drive one of these compared to a brand
new model, especially if the used car is kept at least 4 to 5
years.

To avoid paying too much for a used car or truck, be
sure to check several local newspapers to compare prices
on similar vehicles. Most bookstores and libraries carry
inexpensive used car price guides (see Chapter 10), but
those are merely estimates. What a particular car is worth
depends more on its condition compared to similar cars for
sale in that area and, of course, what people are willing to
pay for them.

When buying from a private party, unless the vehicle is
still covered by the factory warranty, you'll be buying the

vehicle "as is." This means no warranty at all. So, unless you're an experienced auto mechanic, don't ever buy a used car without having *your* mechanic give it a thorough inspection before you sign any contracts or pay any money. You'll have to pay for the inspection, but it's money well-spent, and any problems that are discovered can often be used to negotiate a lower price.

Beware of promises that aren't put in writing. Verbal statements concerning a car's condition (or any warranties) are almost always worthless—if someone won't put it in writing, they probably have no intention of honoring it, and you won't be able to enforce it.

If you are considering the purchase of a used vehicle from a car dealer, keep in mind that many dealers make more money on a used car than a new one, simply because it's much easier for consumers to find out what the dealer's cost is on a new car. The higher the price, the bigger the profit margin, so don't be afraid to offer a lot less than the asking price. It's not unusual for a dealer to make $2,000 to $3,000 profit on a used car selling for $10,000 so there's plenty of room to negotiate.

Most dealers sell their used cars "as is" (without any warranty), and they're not usually very cooperative when it comes to letting people take their vehicles to other shops for prepurchase inspections. Of course, they'll have lots of excuses for those policies. Here are several examples (which are often untrue): "That's not necessary, our mechanics have already done a thorough inspection." "All of our cars are completely safety-checked. They wouldn't be on our lot if they needed any repairs."

While it may be true that a dealer's cars have been "safety-checked" so you're not going to have a steering or brake failure on the way home from the dealership, I seriously doubt that their inspections are very thorough, or done with full disclosure. I've heard too many horror stories from used car buyers to believe otherwise.

You can take advantage of a dealer's reluctance to have his cars inspected by insisting on a warranty. Even though all the used cars on a dealer's lot may have "as is" stickers on the windows, don't forget that practically everything is negotiable when you're buying a car. Tell the salesman, "If the car's condition is as good as you say it is, you shouldn't have any problem giving me a written, bumper-to-bumper 6-month warranty." (Ask for 6 months, settle for three if that's the best deal you can get.)

At this point, the salesman will probably tell you they can't do that (which isn't usually true) and counter with a suggestion that you should buy an extended warranty (for $800 to $1200) if you're so concerned with future repair costs. Extended warranties are negotiable, and they only cost the dealer 30-40% of the amount most people pay for them, so tell the salesman he's going to have to throw in the warranty or you're not going to buy the car.

Here's where you'll probably have to use your "best negotiating weapon" if he says he can't give you any kind of warranty—get up, tell him you're going to find another dealer who's more cooperative, then leave. If he really wants to sell you a car, he'll stop you at the front door, or maybe at the door to your car. Don't let him string you along by promising that "he'll see what he can do"—tell him to throw in the warranty, or you're leaving.

To get the best deal on a car, you'll probably have to terminate the negotiations and walk out at least once before you get what you want. This is often the best way for you to remain in control; if the salesman stays in control, you'll pay too much for the car.

When you start to leave, the salesman may tell you that the price he quoted is only good for that day, and if you come back later, you'll have to pay more for the same car. Your comeback for this line should be: "That's too bad. If you really mean it, I guess I'll have to buy a car from someone else when I'm ready."

Several concluding tips: Know what a car is worth before you decide to buy it. Don't be afraid to walk out if the salesman is playing games, especially if he keeps trying to "bump" the price up. Insist that he treat you with respect and honesty. Unless a dealer lets you get a prepurchase inspection, don't buy a used car from him without some kind of free or low-priced written warranty. If you're buying a used car from a private party, make sure you have *your* mechanic check the car thoroughly *before* you buy it. And if having an extended warranty would help you to sleep at night, be sure to get one at a discount price (see Chapter 5).

CHAPTER 18

What Insiders Have Said

While reading various newspapers, magazines, and trade journals—"gathering intelligence"—I have come across a number of amazing statements made by people inside the auto industry, and a few outside. Some of the brutally-honest statements have created a stir, especially those of insiders saying something negative about leasing—the "savior" of the new car industry.

So, for your reading pleasure, here are some interesting—and educational—quotes from insiders and public figures.

On Leasing

"I believe that the best thing to do is purchase the vehicle outright. Truth in leasing is upon us, and I think once all the facts are out on leasing, people will realize it's not a good thing."
—Chrysler Chairman Robert Eaton
(quoted in *Automotive News*, November 21, 1994)

"I have been in the lease-training business 15 years. I've seen violations of fair-trade practices and downright theft taught to manufacturers and dealers by some of the most reputable and largest lease-training organizations. Cus-

tomers have been bilked of multimillions. Sponsors have turned their backs on deceptive sales practices...federal regulators must take a hard look at those...who created, promoted and continue this grand consumer theft. They've given a black eye to the lease industry."
—President and CEO of lease-training company
(letter to *Automotive News*, January 2, 1995)

"Consumers are getting gouged far too often by unscrupulous auto leasing companies. It's more like auto fleecing than leasing."
—Ralph Nader, consumer advocate
(quoted in the *Detroit Free Press*, October 26, 1994)

"Leasing has become a mode of subsidizing price without being obvious. So much of leasing is another way of discounting and of saying we gouged you in the past."
—Thomas Healey, J.D. Power and Associates partner and director of media services
(quoted in *Automotive News*, April 4, 1994)

"You can play with the numbers anyway you wish, but... for 95% of the American public, leasing isn't the economically intelligent way to go. Rather, it's a means of driving more vehicle than they could otherwise afford...cars, like real estate, are becoming too expensive for the average person to own, so they'll rent them, not because it's best, but because it's the only option."
—Chevrolet dealer on CompuServe, August 28, 1991

On Value Pricing & One-Price Dealers

"I have sold cars for nine years, Oldsmobiles for 1 1/2 years...every time I read or hear that customers are demanding no-haggle, no-hassle, simplified pricing with no

negotiations, I want to scream...customers at both dealerships expect, ask for and sometimes demand negotiations...95 percent are still looking for the lowest price and are shopping for my best deal."
—Oldsmobile sales consultant, Columbus, Ohio
(letter to *Automotive News*, June 12, 1995)

"It is human nature to want to buy a product for the lowest possible price...any retail price set by the manufacturer should be a recommendation only."
—Retired Sales Vice President, General Motors
(letter to *Automotive News*, April 17, 1995)

"About a year and a half ago, we tried one-pricing for a few months, and we took some severe losses. The problem was the competition could beat us by $50."
—Ford dealer, San Jose, California
(quoted in *Automotive News*, February 13, 1995)

"We've found our customers enjoy bargaining...people are suspicious of one-price sales. Also, our customers are people on budgets, and they don't necessarily want all the accessories offered on value-priced vehicles."
—Chevrolet dealer, New Orleans, Louisiana
(quoted in *Automotive News*, February 13, 1995)

"There should be cause for concern about price fixing in our industry...The manufacturers micro-managing a 'value price,' a retail lease price or a fixed 'one-price' vehicle is *price fixing* because it manipulates the market price through *many dealers*...Price fixing, at any level, is always dangerous and anti-competitive...it can hurt the consumer..."
—President, Ford Dealers Alliance, Hackensack, N.J.
(letter to *Automotive News*, December 5, 1994)

"Value pricing was supposed to stop price negotiation. Although some buyers pay the sticker price, more continue to shop for a better deal. Discounting is available on value-priced cars from almost every dealer I have talked to. Even when the dealer's policy is not to discount value-priced cars, the law of supply and demand drives the market price."
—Pontiac dealer in Westminster, California
(letter to *Automotive News*, August 22, 1994)

"It's a marketing gimmick that dealers use, just like red tag sales, Labor Day sales, you name it. And if you say it's going to sweep the nation and it's going to be all one-price dealerships, you're crazy. It's not going to happen."
—Executive vice president
Greater Los Angeles Motor Car Dealers Association
(quote from an Associated Press story printed in
The Long Beach Press-Telegram, September 21, 1992)

On Sales Practices

"What is a rebate? It's the factory's way of saying, 'We know our cars are overpriced, and we don't blame you for not buying. So we'll give you $1,000 or $1,500...' Rebates fan the flames of distrust between customer and dealer. Rebates confess that the sticker price is a joke."
—From an editorial in *Automotive News*, June 5, 1995

"There *must* be a better way to compensate salespersons than the antiquated commission system...Many people equate a visit to a dealership with a visit to the dentist. Why?...Big department stores make shopping a pleasure. Is it a pleasure at your dealership? If not, *why* not?"
—From an editorial in *Automotive News*, March 27, 1995

"Based on traditional price-haggling and sales commissions, 'you couldn't have devised a better pay plan if your intent was to screw the customer.'"
— Charlie Hughes, president
Land Rover North America
(quoted in *Automotive News*, January 16, 1995)

"...how about some ethical standards in advertising? Hey, Detroit, are you listening?...It took a lot of years to build the poor image we have. Does this kind of stuff attract professionals to the business? If manufacturers and dealers keep their heads in the sand, they deserve what they get."
— National sales training manager
(letter to *Automotive News*, May 2, 1994)

"The time is long overdue for this industry—the largest and most important industry in the world—to erase the popular idea that its No. 1 priority is to pull the wool over everyone's eyes."
— From an editorial in *Automotive News*, May 6, 1991

On the New-Car Market

"Prices are rising faster than incomes, and that's not good. It's a warning flag..."
— Jack Smith, president
General Motors
(quoted in the *Detroit Free Press*, February 13, 1995)

"There's no real solution out there. If you lower new car prices, it'll devastate the used car market."
— Tom Webb, chief economist
National Automobile Dealers Association
(quoted in the *Detroit Free Press*, February 13, 1995)

"Retail leasing is a temporary solution that is getting us through the affordability crisis."
—Tom Webb, chief economist
National Automobile Dealers Association
(quoted in *Automotive News*, February 28, 1994)

CHAPTER 19

Dealers & the Media: Blackmail or Censorship?

Why is it that so many consumers have not learned the tricks used by car dealers to make huge profits? Is it because few people know the inside secrets and fewer still are willing to tell the public what they know? Or is it because a serious effort is made to prevent the truth from getting out?

An article I found in the April '92 issue of *Consumer Reports* suggests that the last question is closer to the truth. The article was titled, "Are automobile dealers editing your local newspaper?" and it details the pressure car dealers often put on newspapers to keep them from printing anything dealers may consider "unfavorable."

The *Consumer Reports* article gave specific examples of newspapers that printed wire-service stories on how to bargain when buying a car. A barrage of car dealer complaints on the "lucky" newspapers resulted in an unofficial policy to avoid similar articles in the future. The unlucky newspapers were punished by car dealers who pulled their ads; some papers lost all of their auto advertising for up to six months, until the papers apologized for running the "offending" stories.

Were these just a few isolated incidents, or examples of common practices in the media? To find out, *Consumer Reports* conducted a random survey of 50 daily newspapers, asking editors and writers if local car dealers had any effect on the news. About one-third of the journalists in the survey admitted that they wouldn't run stories on car-buying due to actual (or anticipated) dealer complaints.

One syndicated columnist recently told me that any articles on "how to save money when buying a new car" would only be printed in 50-60% of the papers carrying the column. Another columnist said that any articles car dealers might see as "unfriendly" had to be very carefully worded or most papers wouldn't print them.

The following story is a perfect illustration of the "dealers vs. the media" problem.

1994—Dealers vs. the *San Jose Mercury News*

On May 22, 1994 the *San Jose Mercury News* (a major newspaper in the San Francisco Bay area) ran a story titled, "A Car Buyer's Guide to Sanity." The article gave readers tips on how to negotiate lower prices with car dealers and included information on how to find out what the dealer's cost was on a particular model. A specific car buying service was also mentioned, with an explanation of how they force dealers to bid against each other, a process designed to get the lowest possible price. [The two services that received the best reviews in the article were Fighting Chance and CarBargains, both recommended by me in this book.]

The next day, local dealers complained about the article, so a meeting between the publisher and about three dozen dealers was set for May 25. According to the executive editor of the *Mercury News*, the dealers were upset by the "tone" of the article, citing three "offensive" quotes that were printed. One quote came from the president of the car buying service, who said that the "real power of information is that it keeps the dealers honest." Another quote came from the founder and president of Fighting Chance, who said, "One reason God gave you feet was so you could use them to walk away from car salesmen." [That one is my personal favorite.]

According to the president of the local dealers' association, dealers were insulted by the tone of the article, claiming they were portrayed as being unethical. One dealer claimed that the article said they take advantage of people. [I'm sure that's never happened!]

At the meeting, the publisher was reported to have defended the article and the reporter who wrote it. Several weeks later, over 40 dealers pulled their advertising from the paper, saying they were upset with the arrogant attitude of the *Mercury News*. [What nerve that paper had, deciding what to print without asking their advertisers first. Who do they think they are, anyway?]

Local dealers denied that the cancelled ads were part of a coordinated effort, but the newspaper got the message, nonetheless. (Estimates of lost advertising revenue were at least $1 million.) Newspaper officials took steps to patch things up with the dealers, publishing follow-up stories that implied that the (offending) article was not well-written. They also ran a full-page color ad promoting area dealers, encouraging readers to purchase cars from them.

The fence-mending efforts of the *Mercury News* paid off. By early July, some of the dealers had returned as advertisers and more were expected within the next few months. According to the president of the dealers' association, they returned because of the paper's efforts to mend relations with the dealers and, ironically, *because they had no other viable alternative for advertising.* [The cancelled ads probably hurt the dealers more than the newspaper.]

Due to the actions taken by newspaper officials, fellow reporters felt that the writer had been discredited. They also were concerned that it looked like the newspaper had caved in to pressure from advertisers. [No, not at all!] The writer also said he would think twice before covering another auto topic.

Enter the Federal Trade Commission

After a story about the *Mercury News* situation appeared in the *Washington Post*, the Federal Trade Commission opened an investigation to determine whether the local car dealers violated federal laws that prohibit anticompetitive agreements. The FTC is particularly interested in a dealer meeting held at the San Jose Hyatt Hotel shortly after dealers met with *Mercury News* officials. (Advertising cancellations started soon after the dealer meeting.)

The issue: When the dealers pulled their advertising, were they (in effect) agreeing not to compete, and did their actions depress competition in the local area? The FTC is not challenging the right of dealers to stop advertising, or to punish newspapers for running articles they dislike. Whether actions were taken that restricted competition is the issue.

The president of the local dealers' association denies that the dealers acted together in pulling their ads. [I'm sure it was just a coincidence.]

In an unrelated case, the FTC completed an investigation of the Arizona Automobile Dealers Association regarding possible antitrust violations. On June 3, 1994, without admitting guilt, the association signed a consent agreement that promised to eliminate restrictions prohibiting discount advertising. The association represents about 99 percent of the new car and truck dealers in the state and had a "Standards for Advertising Motor Vehicles" policy that prohibited ads such as "we'll beat any price."

Dealers vs. Buffalo (NY) TV Station?

On February 15, 1995 ABC's *PrimeTime Live* aired a show on new-car leasing scams, using hidden cameras and a female reporter posing as a customer. In the show, *PrimeTime* accused a number of dealers of trying to overcharge on leases. (See Chapter 1 for details of the show.)

According to a *USA Today* story from February 20, one station—WKBW in Buffalo—preempted the *PrimeTime* auto-leasing show. One hour of *Roseanne* reruns was aired instead. The article said, "Word around ABC News is that local car dealers pressured the station to yank the show for the night."

ATTEMPTS TO SUPPRESS THIS INFO--

I have experienced similar "censorship" in radio and newspapers while spreading the word about my first book. Although many radio stations have let me do interviews, a significant percentage of them would not allow me to name any of the well-known auto repair companies that had been charged with fraudulent business practices. And most stations did not want me to say anything at all about car dealers. Why not? *Because they were big advertisers.*

My radio show was cancelled on one station after I mentioned a national auto repair chain that had a number of recent undercover busts. Why? *Because a shop from that very chain was a major advertiser on the station.* (Since then, that same company has been accused of selling unnecessary repairs following undercover investigations in two more states, and is now the target of a national class-action, consumer fraud lawsuit.)

Newspaper editors have asked me to write articles on

auto repair scams, but they wouldn't allow me to include names of companies that were charged with fraudulent business practices after undercover investigations. Why not? *Because they were advertisers.*

It should be obvious by now why so many people never learn "what car dealers don't want you to know"—the information is not allowed in many newspapers, or on many radio and TV stations.

Until more newspapers, radio, and TV stations develop the integrity and backbone that is necessary to stand up to automotive advertisers, they will continue to get away with keeping "unfavorable" information out of the public eye. Because many consumers won't learn how to protect themselves, they'll continue to be victimized by "slick" car salesmen.

THE SOLUTION--

As you can imagine, there will be many attempts to keep the car-buying secrets in this book from becoming common knowledge. So do your friends a favor—if you think this information will save them money, tell them about it.

Summary

By now, you've probably learned more than you ever wanted to know about the new car business. And even if you only skimmed through the book, you know a lot more than most dealers would like. But don't assume that all dealers and salesmen are dishonest, because they're not. I just exposed all the dirty tricks so you can tell the good guys from the bad. When you do find an honest dealer, tell all your friends — they'll appreciate it, and so will the dealer.

The secret to getting the best price is competition based on information. Find out how big the profit margin is on a car, then make the dealers compete against each other so you end up with the lowest possible price. When you're done, you'll know you got a good deal.

Don't get into arguments over how much profit a dealer "should make," that's for him to decide, not you or me, not the car manufacturers, not the government. I just thought you should know that dealers do sell cars at huge discounts that aren't advertised — *they just don't want you to know.*

And don't feel bad if a dealer only makes a small profit on your car. Chances are the next customer (who hasn't read this book) will more than make up for it.

Another consumer book by

Mark Eskeldson

What Auto Mechanics
Don't Want You to Know

LEARN ALL ABOUT:

Secret Warranties:
How to Get Free Repairs

Undercover Investigations:
Which Well-Known Repair Shops Have Been Busted

Avoiding Repair Scams;
Getting Your Money Back

Finding Mechanics You Can Trust

Vehicle Maintenance Secrets

"...a better-informed consumer is less likely to be taken
advantage of. And that's why Eskeldson wrote his
book...Even if you don't have the time to spend reading...keep the book as a reference."
— *CAR AND DRIVER*

Technews Publishing, $11.95
ISBN 0-9640560-0-3

Both books available in bookstores
or call (800) 247-6553
All orders shipped within 48 hours
Money-back Guarantee